The Best of
Cutler Anderson
Architects

ROCKPORT

Foreword by James Cutler
Introduction by Sheri Olson

Text by Alicia Kennedy, Theresa Morrow, and Sheri Olson

BEVERLY MASSACHUSETTS

ROCKPORT PUBLISHERS

The Best of
Cutler Anderson
Architects

First published in the United States of America by
Rockport Publishers, a member of
Quayside Publishing Group
100 Cummings Center
Suite 406-L
Beverly, Massachusetts 01915-6101
Telephone: (978) 282-9590
Fax: (978) 283-2742
www.rockpub.com

ISBN-13: 978-1-59253-405-0
ISBN-10: 1-59253-405-8

10 9 8 7 6 5 4 3 2 1

Art Director: Alicia Kennedy
Design: Chris Grimley for over,under

Cover image: Ohana House at Niulii
Back cover image: Orlean Gillespie Residence
Photographs by Art Grice

Some of the material in this book first appeared in *James Cutler* (*Contemporary World Architects* series), published by Rockport Publishers in 1997, and in *Cutler Anderson Architects*, by Sheri Olson, published by Rockport Publishers in 2004.

Printed in China

CONTENTS

THE CASE FOR A TANGIBLE REALITY:
FOREWORD BY JAMES CUTLER

Sitting on the upper deck of the ferry that travels from my Bainbridge Island home to Seattle, I ponder the future of architecture and wonder if architects have lost touch with core values. It's an unusually sunny day in late December, and a fiddler plays in the corner of the sheltered area while high-pitched children's voices mingle with the low pitch of adults in quiet conversation. The ferry engine hums steadily in the background, and the hull pushes aside the water with a gentle sound. The low winter sun sparkles silver off the water, and the dark north face of Mount Rainier, sixty miles away, looms over this picture, reminding us of our position in the landscape. What does this delightful scene have to do with architecture? Everything. I feel architects can capture and illuminate these moments of visual and acoustic pleasure that elicit emotional and memorable responses.

I often find myself surprised and moved by a photographer's ability to capture moments of beauty that might, at first glance, appear mundane or go unnoticed. A stick on the beach or a pattern of stones can be transformed by the way a photograph reveals the subject's essence. Architecture can also reflect and reveal the unique characteristics of materials and places. Beginning with the assumption that everything—from objects to people, from events to institutions—has a nature or spirit, architecture can reveal this spirit in a way that is as tangible as this pleasant winter scene.

From the Seattle ferry terminal, I meander up to Pike Place Public Market. This conglomeration of nineteenth- and early-twientieth-century buildings forms a vertical edge between downtown and the waterfront. I buy fresh bread, Spanish cheese, and a little basket of out-of-season raspberries and sit on a bench in the main arcade. Cold air permeates the market but has not deterred the weekend crowds of shoppers, tourists, musicians, and fishmongers, all enjoying this urban show. Like many people, I love the market. It is a tangible conduit for people to connect emotionally with the city and the region. It also elevates the everyday experience of shopping and more truly reveals the actual social nature of "market." The directness of the experience—the barter and banter with merchants and craftspeople, the careful arrangement of produce and crafts, the presence of crowds and shoppers—connects us to the fundamental essence of the institution of commerce. The experience is genuine, and we respond to it in a way not matched by the automated checkout at the supermarket.

This example of an institution revealing its true nature and, thus, creating an emotional and memorable response is more than applicable to our profession. It is not clear to me that we, as a profession, see or value this. It is difficult to listen to the voices of every social and material component of a circumstance and produce a design that allows them to sing in harmony. It is much easier to pick up on a narrowly focused topical abstraction or a technological marvel and run with it, ignoring the tangible realities of region, place, materials, and even institutions.

I'm home now. The weather has turned. The wind is howling through the fir trees on the edge of my bluff. The gusts carry with them a horizontal rain that is pelting the windows. The rain and wind have gathered their energy far out in the North Pacific and are expending it against my trees and house. Immense thermal forces generated thousands of miles from here are knocking on my windows to remind me that the small place where I live is connected to the whole planet and is subject to its forces.

Inside, it's calm. The cats are sleeping on their respective turfs. There's a low fire in the ill-scaled stone fireplace. In the bookshelves above the fireplace is a book entitled *Life*. The author, Richard Fortey, who was the chief paleontologist of the British Museum, traces in a mere four hundred pages the history of life for the past two billion years! This synopsis of the broad sweep of evolution concludes with a photo of rows and rows of slot machines. The photo is used to illustrate that we are the product of a million times a million almost random chances, possibly more chances than the number of stars in our galaxy. Fortey makes it clear that we were not inevitable. At each occurrence in the history of life, things could have gone a different way. Given the enormous compounded number of events that created us, it is probable that we are unique in the universe. There almost certainly is other life out there, but something that sees, perceives, and feels the world around it in the way we do is highly unlikely. For all

we know, we may be the only living thing in the universe that feels emotion or sees beauty. Our rational and emotional cognition of the world around us is what makes us human. It is a gift beyond measure.

Given this singular ability, I would argue that responding to, revealing, reflecting, and protecting the uniqueness of the real world around us should be our highest calling. Choreographing the visual experience of individuals so that the most poignant photos of a particular set of circumstances are revealed gives viewers the opportunity to understand the world around them, not only on an intellectual but on the more important emotional human level. These emotional responses connect us strongly to the world, and in this memorable way, they open the doors for us to feel and love—in essence, they remind us of the gift of cognition.

In a world in which the sheer pressure of human population growth is devouring our biodiversity and changing our atmospheric chemistry to the point of radically altering our climate, there may be great value in employing an ethic that guides people to an emotional connection to reality. I know of no one who is in favor of these ongoing environmental alterations or is looking forward to the unpredictable consequences. I also know of no one who feels the planet will be a better place to live two hundred years from now. Yet, why do we do little or nothing about changing this potentially unpleasant future?

Even though the answers to this question may be politically complex, I feel the core of our problem lies in our fundamental disconnection from the living world that sustains us. We, as a culture, no longer have the primitive emotional

knowledge that we and the rest of the living world are one. We may not be able to do anything about this loss and its concomitant problems, but if there is a path that avoids the looming future, it will start from an ethic of respect, appreciation, and love for all the variety of this planet. That love can only be fostered by first promoting an emotional connection to the world. Where our hearts go, our minds and actions will follow.

Therefore, I feel any methodology in any craft or profession that reinforces an emotional recognition of the gift of the real world is valuable in defending a future in which, it is hoped, other people can enjoy the world howling through Douglas firs.

2003

OUT OF THE WOODS:
INTRODUCTION BY SHERI OLSON

The work of the architectural design firm Cutler Anderson bears witness to the proverbial tree falling in the forest. Like the surveys they undertake at the beginning of each design, their work stakes a place in the world from which nature becomes visible. They believe that to know nature is to love it and to love it is to fight for its preservation. Nature is a complex word and, according to Raymond Williams, a history of its uses would be a large part of the history of human thought. For Jim Cutler and Bruce Anderson, the definition is simple: Nature is that part of the world that sustains humanity physically, emotionally, and spiritually. In this regard, architecture is problematic in that it devours unspoiled land and raw materials at an alarming rate. The logical conclusion is not to build unless you believe that beauty does not reside in objects but is in the eye of the beholder—thus leaving it open to manipulation. In essence, a building can help people see the forest in spite of the trees—and, for Cutler Anderson, this is the purpose of architecture: the realization of nature.

Ironically, Cutler Anderson is not considered "green" enough for many of the green architects who hold conferences in convention centers and officially designate the like-minded with special certification. At a time when this well-intentioned movement often produces earnest but uninspiring buildings, the firm makes an important point that emotions rally people faster than facts. A thousand projects with recycled carpet have less impact than one that reveals the beauty of the natural world.

Jim Cutler's sensitivity to the environment traces to his childhood in Kingston, Pennsylvania, a blue-collar coal-mining town surrounded by slag heaps. The son of a Russian immigrant who worked in a family-owned clothing store, Jim spent his childhood combing the woods for mushrooms; there he learned to be an acute observer of nature. At the University of Pennsylvania, Cutler won a coveted spot in Louis I. Kahn's postgraduate studio—the last Kahn taught before his death. On a personal level, the attention of one of the masters of twentieth-century architecture was an important validation of his talent, but, more importantly, Kahn taught Cutler how to think. He continues to approach design through the Socratic method Kahn used to explore the "existence of will"—the essence of a material and its highest and best use. Cutler continues where Kahn left off when he speaks of honoring the trees felled to build a house. Otherwise, his wood-frame and glass designs appear on the surface to have little in common with Kahn's monumental brick and stone architecture. A closer look reveals Kahn's influence in Cutler Anderson's disciplined plans and the spiritual quality of space.

Where Jim Cutler breaks with his mentor is in Kahn's rejection of nature: "What man makes, nature can not make." In this regard, Cutler shares more with Le Corbusier and his deurbanization projects of the 1930s and 1940s, which sought a return to the conditions where people could contemplate and enjoy nature. This is key to understanding that Cutler Anderson's work is not confined to the woods.

A road trip brought Cutler to the Pacific Northwest in the early 1970s and to the balance between nature and culture—Bainbridge Island's forest of firs and rocky beaches is only half an hour by ferry to downtown Seattle—that ties him to this place. He founded James Cutler Architects on the island in 1977. The firm's work first came to national attention with a 1986 American Institute of Architects National Honor Award for the Parker Residence, built inside a recycled fishnet-drying shed. The project marks the beginning of what collaborator Peter Bohlin calls a progression from derivative to more personal designs.

Around this time, a former design student from a class Cutler taught at the University of Washington in Seattle, Bruce Anderson, joined the firm. He became a partner in 2001, and the firm's name changed to Cutler Anderson Architects. Well suited to their respective roles, the poet and the pragmatist, Cutler initiates conceptual ideas and works with Anderson to develop and refine them using a design shorthand developed through more than twenty years of working together. A Pacific Northwest native, Anderson's experience as planning commission chair and president of the Bainbridge Island Land Trust broadens the scope and reach of the firm, making him key in the firm's pursuit of public projects. Now a thirteen-person office, the firm is on the second floor of a converted boathouse on a Bainbridge Island marina, a short walk to the ferry to Seattle across Elliott Bay.

A breakthrough project in the theoretical development of the firm is the Virginia Merrill Bloedel Education Center on Bainbridge Island (1992). The poetry of this undertaking—the building memorializes the client's sixty-two years of marriage with a view of his wife's unmarked grave—resonated with the architects, and it was here they began their quest to honor felled trees with a design that displays every piece of wood. Here, Cutler Anderson began fully to articulate the relationship between architecture and nature with detailing that heightens awareness of materials and, by extension, the natural world.

Out of Bloedel came the commission of a lifetime, a house for one of the richest men in the world, Bill Gates. Cutler Anderson, the only local firm invited to compete for the commission, joined forces with Peter Bohlin (as a graduate student, Cutler built models in Bohlin's Wilkes-Barre office) to win the 40,000-square-foot (3,716-square-meter) complex on Lake Washington near Microsoft's Redmond campus. The project gave the firm name recognition beyond the Pacific Northwest and the budget to experiment. The emphasis moves away from skin, seen in the earlier houses, to skeleton, as the architects restate the meaning of wall, post, and beam and their interrelation in space. The primacy of structure and the almost infinite variety of expression is shown in the multiple and subtle detailing of column and beam connections.

As with any project of this scope and stature, the Gates complex had its price, consuming the Cutler Anderson office for seven years. Potential clients went on a wait list until the project was finished, while others did not call because they

thought the firm catered only to the extraordinarily rich. It was also a philosophical crisis for Cutler Anderson as they struggled to reconcile the vast consumption of natural resources in the Gates house—especially wood—with Cutler's reverence for trees. The project brought home the inherent critique of capitalism embodied by the green movement; it is no coincidence that the 1999 World Trade Organization riots occurred in Seattle, home of Microsoft, Boeing, and Starbucks. This may or may not explain why Gates chose Cutler Anderson for his architect (perhaps as a means to mend the rift between globalism and the environment on a personal level?) but, more likely, explains Cutler's current ambivalence about the project.

One client who waited was Barbara Wood. Her house (1998), on rural Vashon Island, Washington, is a seminal project for Cutler Anderson as they sought ways to achieve an articulated design on more modest budgets. Built-up sections of light wood framing and steel plates replace the heavy timber structure used at the Gates house. The literalness of exposing every piece of wood is also gone, replaced by glimpses of framing in key places as the drywall stops short of the floor and the ceiling or is cut larger around windows to give every stud its due. The real discovery is in the greenhouse, where a concern about condensation led the architects to bolt standard window frames on the outside face of the wood framing. This frees the relationship between window and structure and marks the beginning of the layered transparency that is now the firm's hallmark.

These ideas were pushed to an extreme at Tanglefoot (2001), a house on a remote lake in Idaho for an inventor and

his young family. The house represents an unusually close collaboration between Cutler Anderson and the client, who hunted down an aluminum tape (used in the aerospace industry) that enabled the refinement of the window system first used at the Wood residence. At Tanglefoot, aluminum bars and channels hold entire walls of glass away from the wood framing on aluminum spacers. The house is baroque in its fecundity, with multiple layers of wood framing inside mirroring the richness of the wilderness outside.

The pendulum swings the other way, toward spareness, with the Pine Forest Cabin (1999) in the semiarid forest of Methow Valley, Washington. On either side of a long wood platform, two balloon-framed walls continue unclad past the building envelope to stretch space beyond the plan. The precision and control of the detailing underscore the light, ephemeral quality of the structure.

The firm's first major public project, a branch library designed in collaboration with Johnston Architects for Maple Valley, Washington (2001), shows how these ideas can transcend the domestic world and are, in turn, transformed by the transition from private to public. Without the budget or programmatic freedom of a house, time and effort focus on the essentials: simple geometries, structural clarity, and the connection to place. Like the houses, the library challenges conventions (the forest wasn't clear-cut to make room for a parking lot; instead, cars are slipped between trees) and creates personal places within a larger shared space.

These ideas and the methodology also ring true in the firm's first urban project, a branch library (also in collaboration with

Johnston Architects) in Seattle's densest city neighborhood. With its monolithic brick walls, hollowed-out interior, and distinction between functional and honorific spaces, the Capitol Hill Library (2003) is overtly reminiscent of Kahn's 1972 library at Phillips Exeter Academy in New Hampshire. But Cutler Anderson makes this library entirely their own, covering the walls and wrapping the interior with a vine-covered trellis that creates a vertical oasis in the city.

Grace Church (2003) on Bainbridge Island is the culmination of Cutler Anderson's investigations and intentions to date. It recalls the structural expressiveness and spiritual quality of Gothic cathedrals with exposed wood, articulated connections, and layers of glass. The spiritual connects to the secular through the gravitational forces made visible in the structure and in the big leaf maple framed by the sanctuary. Asked for an explanation of the design for the church's dedication, Cutler wrote, "God is manifest in the physics of the world." For him, there is no distinction between form and content or between object and meaning, just as Susan Sontag wrote in *Against Interpretation* that modern art "should need no interpretation because whatever meaning it had was immanent in the sensory experience of the work." The firm holds this idea so dear that they, along with artist and collaborator Maggie Smith, brought a successful suit against the city of Salem, Massachusetts, to have an interpretive plaque removed from the Salem Witch Trials Tercentenary Memorial (1992). The memorial speaks eloquently for itself and the twenty innocent victims through the experience of the materials, trees, and space just as the cast bronze

letters at the Armed Forces Memorial in Norfolk, Virginia (2000), give voice to the sacrifices made by servicemen and women who lost their lives in war. Memorials are an important part of the firm's work, providing the visual clues that can turn keys in locked hearts and release emotions in a rational world. For Cutler Anderson, architecture is the means for establishing the passionate connections—to the past, a place, and other people—that can change the world.

2004

PROJECTS

Parker Residence

BAINBRIDGE ISLAND, WASHINGTON

Built inside the shell of a 1920s net-drying shed, this shingle-style building evolved to address its industrial harbor context. Because the building was positioned at the toe of a 12-foot (3.7-meter) embankment, the entry needed to be located on the second level, while logic dictated that the living (public) area be placed at dock level. The architects felt that the stair from the entry to the living level should be generous enough to invite guests down while still providing a sense of enclosure so that the stair did not feel precipitous. To achieve this balance, the stair was narrowed at the top and flared at the bottom.

The variety of natural woods—fir floors, hemlock walls, fir cabinetry, cedar shingle walls and roof—is worked to highlight how they are joined together in the construction process. The interior of the building is structured to carry the second floor while still keeping a vestige of the initial shed volume. Separating the bedroom spaces from the entry by raising them two steps up allows privacy for these rooms, yet leaves them open to the volume. The building is heated by a low-temperature, salt-water-to-freshwater heat pump that minimizes energy consumption.

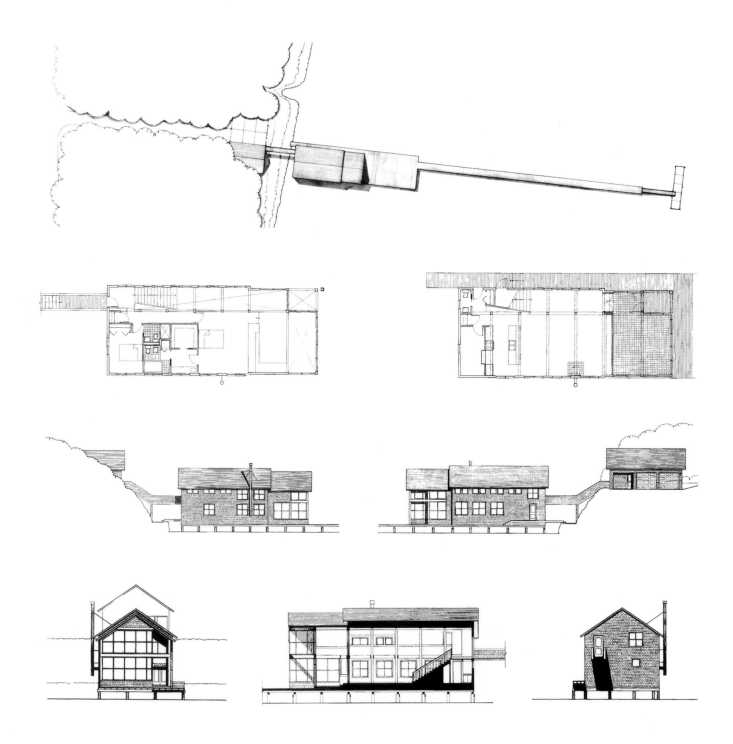

The functional spaces of the house run lengthwise, with a two-story sunroom replacing the area where fishnets once hung to dry. Carefully placed clerestories let in light, and a former storage loft upstairs is transformed into bedrooms, bathrooms, and a den. The slightly twisted stairway at the entrance invites guests to descend to the lower living area, while maintaining a sense of enclosure.

The Bridge House

BAINBRIDGE ISLAND, WASHINGTON

Environmental concerns came first in this residence, which spans a seasonal stream on a heavily wooded parcel of land on Bainbridge Island, Washington. Initially, the land was thought to be unbuildable, its half-acre (0.2 hectares) bisected by a ravine and stream. The client had already received a permit to culvert the stream and build a colonial residence, but after some discussion, was convinced to give up such an environmentally destructive scheme.

Built over the stream, the Bridge House was intended to set an example for a more sensitive response to the land. Beyond reducing the building's footprint, the architects made an effort to design the construction process to limit collateral damage to the terrain.

The building itself spans 42 feet (12.8 meters) across the stream between its concrete-block abutments. All the footings were hand-dug and the spanning floor deck was used as a staging area. By eliminating plywood, plasterboard, and paints, the house was built free of formaldehydes, thus creating a nontoxic structure.

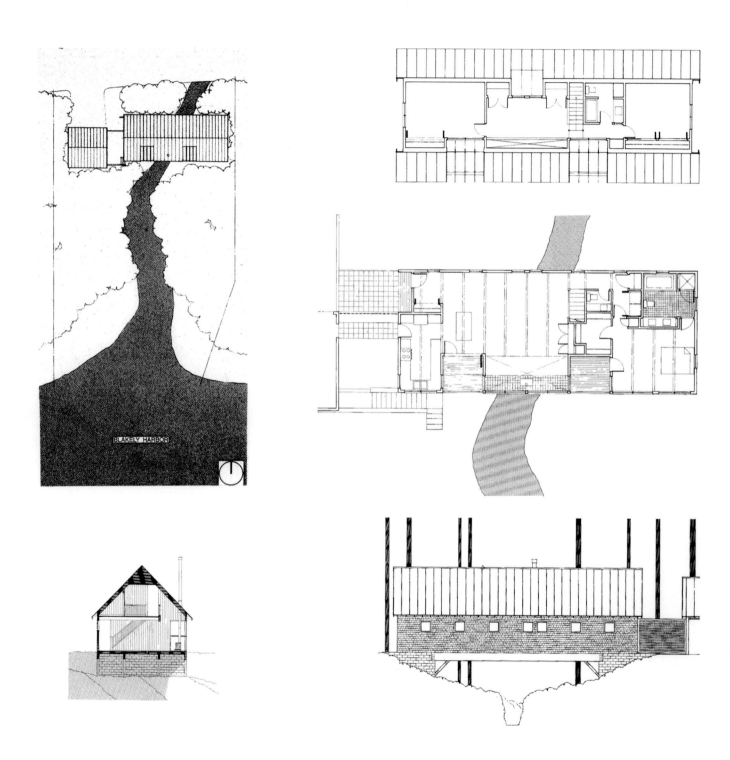

BLAKELY HARBOR

The bridge over the wooded ravine enables the house to have as little impact on the environment as possible. The building tucks carefully into the alder, cedar, and fir woods. (Only one tree was felled during construction.) Two covered balconies have galvanized railings.

The house is all wood construction except for the steel-reinforced, broken face concrete-block abutment for the bridge. Fir-wrapped windows open up the view toward the waterfront. The kitchen cabinets are solid fir with a natural finish, and natural pine boards were used for the building's walls and floors. Glass blocks in the hearth of the wood stove give a view of the stream beneath the house.

Wright Guesthouse

THE HIGHLANDS, WASHINGTON

Part of an 8.5-acre (3.4-hectare) complex owned by art collectors, this guest-house nestles into the landscape and remains invisible from the main residence. To integrate the structure into the landscape, the guesthouse is fitted into a natural depression in the surrounding forest. In fact, it is dug into the depression as much as 14 feet (4.3 meters) below grade. The residence is accessed both by a sculpture trail from the main house and by a boardwalk through the forest.

By emphasizing the massive concrete wall, the architects attempted to reveal the weight of the earth and the weight of the materials used to retain it. The concrete also creates a visual contrast with the wooded "tent" that encloses the residence. Inside, the warm, gray-green concrete walls of the house serve as a foil for paintings and sculpture.

The wooded structure was twisted from the L-shaped concrete wall both to enlarge the entrance and to constrict the elbow where the circulation passes from public to private zones. This misalignment of grids further heightens the contrast between the ephemeral wooden tent and the timeless concrete wall.

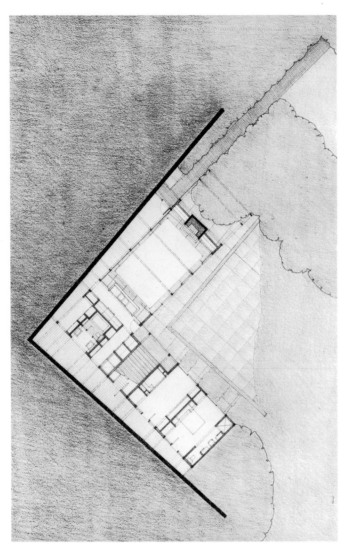

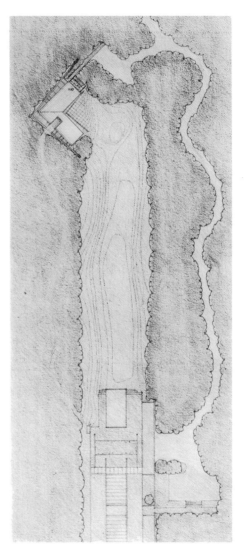

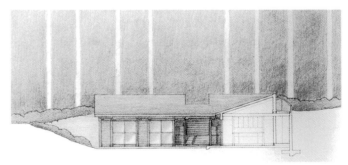

A secondary stairway rises within a protected alcove along the building's west elevation. Arcades composed of heavy-timber "trees" define the north and south elevations. The stairway and bold wooden arcades take the place of grand interior lobbies, functioning as a transition between indoors and out.

The living-room hearth is twisted on the concrete floor. Broken concrete echoes the outside wall design. Fir woodwork contrasts with the gray concrete walls inside, again suggesting a balance of transient present with continuing past. The L-shaped guesthouse's outer concrete wall, fir framing, and cedar siding are fitted into the surrounding forest.

The approach to the house is through a skylit entry deck; the light from inside glows on the interior fir walls. Fiberglass ceiling panels extend the length of the hallways, serving as a gasket between the wooden building and the concrete wall. The wall and house are not aligned, creating an entryway that tapers to a narrow passage. The wide end of the entry leads to the public spaces in the house, the narrow to the more private areas.

Virginia Merrill Bloedel Education Center

BAINBRIDGE ISLAND, WASHINGTON

Located on the 150-acre (60.7-hectare) Bloedel Reserve on Bainbridge Island, Washington, a building that will ultimately be a lecture hall began life as a memorial to the owner's sixty-two years of marriage. The eighty-nine-year-old client, owner of a semipublic estate of gardens, asked for a building with a view of his wife's unmarked grave, located at the end of an existing reflecting pool.

The stone supports of the future Education Center were set on axis with the gravesite. Exposed heavy-timber posts and beams carry the structural load. Stone plinths support the superstructure, which spans an intermittent water course. The entry walk centers the axis through the building to a viewing deck, from whence it continues through the woods into an open meadow. Here the axial line is marked by a boulder before it goes on to reach the poolside gravesite.

The owner's bedroom is twisted so that his bed is also aligned on axis with the gravesite. The stone and wooden structure of the 1,400-square-foot (130-square-meter) building is carefully fitted into its forest context. The organic wooden structure will someday decay, but the stone elements will remain as a symbol of the owner's relationship with his wife.

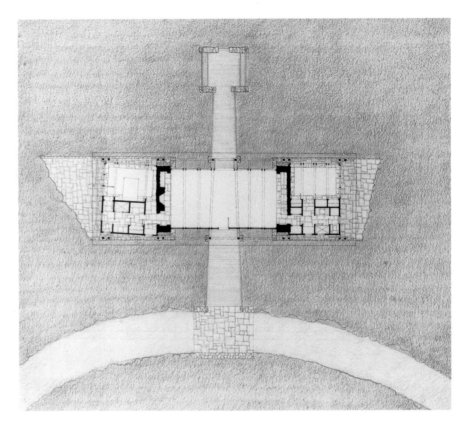

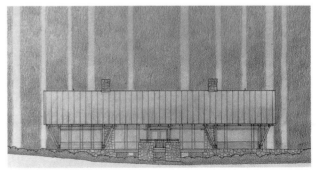

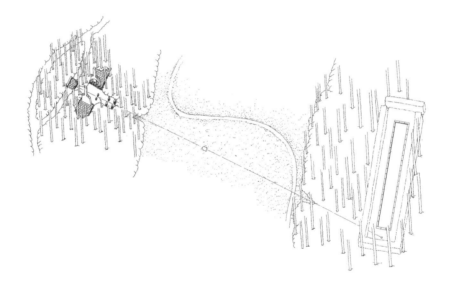

The beams at the central doorway are doubled, symbolizing the couple's long partnership. The wooden deck, supported by large stone piers, carries the axis toward the gravesite.

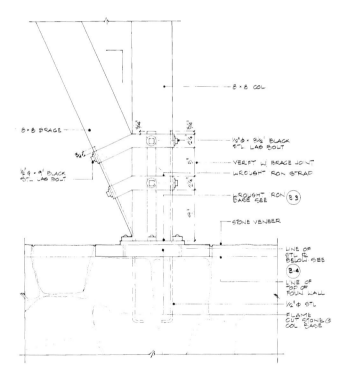

The drawing is labeled with the following annotations:

- 8 × 8 COL
- 8 × 8 BRACE
- 1/2"∅ × 9" BLACK STL LAG BOLT
- 1/2"∅ × 3 1/2" BLACK STL LAG BOLT
- VERIFY W/ BRACE JOINT
- WROUGHT IRON STRAP
- WROUGHT IRON BASE SEE (B-3)
- STONE VENEER
- LINE OF STL PL BELOW SEE (B-4)
- LINE OF TOP OF FOUN WALL
- 1/2"∅ STL
- FLAME CUT STONE @ COL BASE

Exposed heavy-timber posts and beams carry the structural load. Stone plinths support the superstructure.

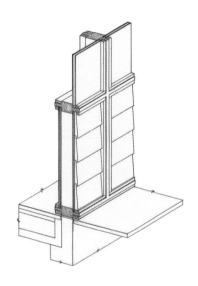

Inside the building, paired stone arches reinforce the symmetry of the gravesite axis. At opposite ends of the room, stone walls with inset doorways echo the stone piers that support the building.

Two bedroom suites at each end of the building will eventually become guest rooms for visiting lecturers. The architects designed the furniture to fit with the revealed wood structure.

Salem Witch Trials Tercentenary Memorial

SALEM, MASSACHUSETTS

The Salem Witch Trials Tercentenary Memorial attempts to give form to concepts of injustice. The architects worked with artist Maggie Smith, winning an international competition for the design of the memorial in 1991. The memorial commemorates the trial and execution of twenty innocent people suspected of witchcraft in 1692. Situated on a 5,000-square-foot (464.5-square-meter) plot surrounded by a seventeenth-century cemetery—in which many of the citizens of the 1692 community are buried—the memorial features a wall from which earth has been dug out, making visitors feel as if they are standing in an actual grave.

The designers approached the idea of injustice through four words: Silence, Deafness, Persecution, and Memory. To represent silence, they graded and organized the site to emphasize the surrounding tombstones as mute watchers looking into the memorial. For deafness, they inscribed the historical protests of innocence on the entry threshold and had them slide under the stone wall in mid-sentence. For persecution, they planted black locust trees, from which the accused were believed to be hanged. For memory, they inscribed the names, dates, and manners of death on stone slabs, which were then cantilevered from the stone wall as benches.

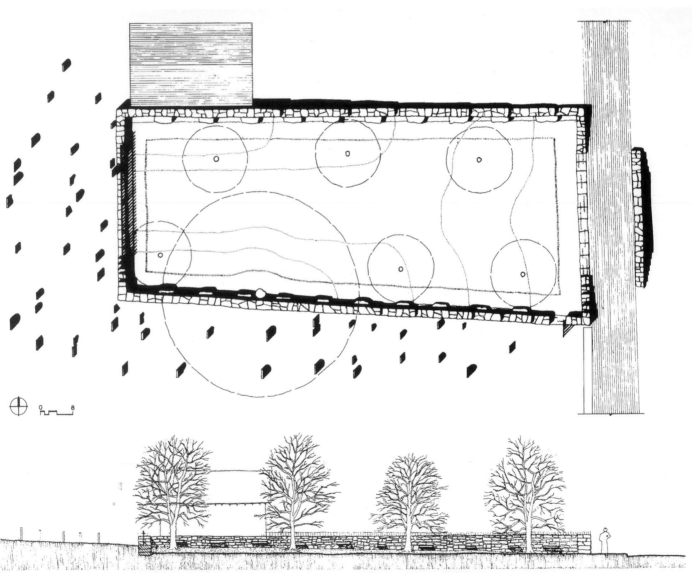

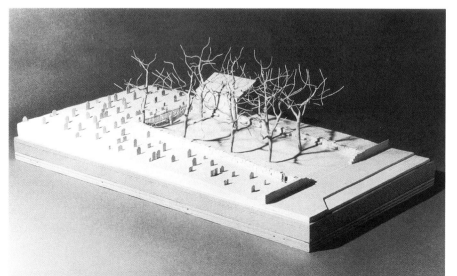

Protestations of innocence mark the threshold to the memorial. The victims' words, which run under the stone wall in mid-sentence—symbolizing the crushed truth—were taken from court records. Tombstones in the adjacent cemetery mark the resting places of the victims' neighbors. A barred iron fence and rough granite walls divide the cemetery from the memorial, emphasizing the confrontation of persecutors and victims.

51

The wall of the memorial was formed of weathered granite, taken from an abandoned New Hampshire quarry. The pieces were put in place with crowbars and wedges, much like the farm fences of years past. The twenty stone benches around the perimeter are inscribed with the victims' names and execution dates. These are the first markers for the victims in three hundred years. A seventeenth-century typeface was used for the inscriptions.

Paulk Residence

SEABECK, WASHINGTON

Perched on a 200-foot (61-meter) waterfront bluff, the Paulk residence commands a strong view of the Olympic Mountains, despite being nestled in a dense forest. Fitted into the woods on the remnants of an old logging road, the house is anchored to the ground at its south end, then floats 15 feet (4.6 meters) high as the ground falls away beneath it at the north end.

Faced with a required 80-foot (24.4-meter) setback from the edge of an upward-sloping bluff, the architects captured the view by allowing the building to rise out of grade as it moves east. A 130-foot (39.6-meter) entry ramp passes through the building, emerging from the opposite side to lead to a belvedere high over the cliff. Since the land was relatively undisturbed by construction (only three trees were felled), the bridge offers guests an intimate experience of the forest as they move through it.

On the inside, the ceiling is pulled back in places to reveal the nature of the construction materials. Framing in the foyer is exposed; floor joists are cut at random lengths; sheet metal is screwed into place as soffits or wall panels.

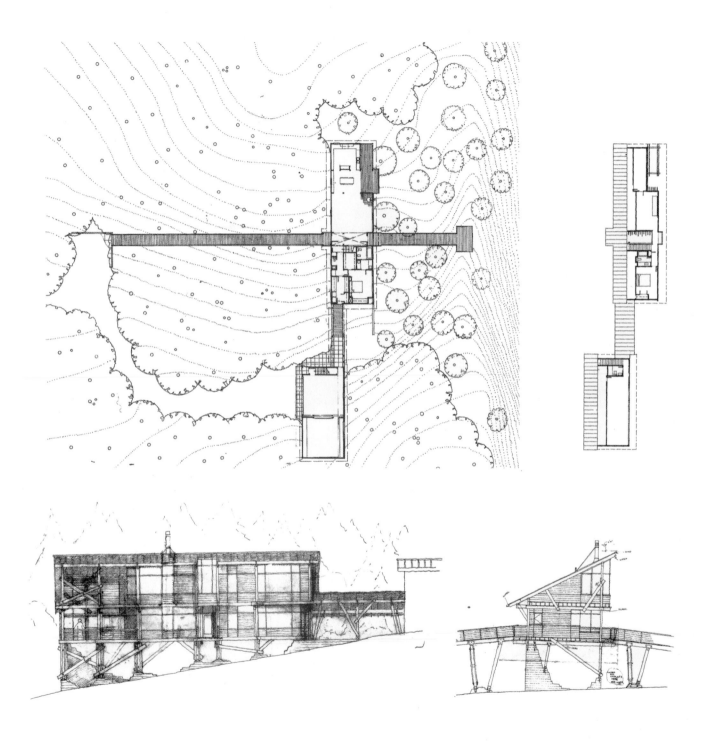

The long wooden ramp leading to the entrance accommodates a site of perverse contours. The bridge is supported by wood posts on concrete plinths, and the entry door is surrounded by glass.

Construction was designed to create minimal disturbance of the forest. At one point, the roof and rafters were notched to preserve a tree. The haphazard, cross-braced posts under the house are expressive of the ad hoc nature of the support.

A 22-foot (6.7-meter)-tall grid of glass reveals a landscape of trees and water. Each of the nine rooms, except for the laundry, has a view.

To highlight the materials used in construction, the ceiling is pulled back in places to reveal the rafters and the framing is exposed. Maple floors and pine paneling are treated with a transparent white stain.

Guesthouse

MEDINA, WASHINGTON

Situated at the high end of a steep, suburban lot on Lake Washington near Seattle, this 1,700-square-foot (158-square-meter) guesthouse was the first in a compound of buildings designed to combine state-of-the-art computer technology with environmental sensitivity. A joint venture with Peter Bohlin of Bohlin Cywinski Jackson, the complex includes a reception pavilion to seat one hundred twenty, a boathouse, a movie theater, a trampoline room, a swimming pool, and a twenty-car garage, in addition to the main residence.

The intent was to test managerial, aesthetic, and structural systems in this initial building before continuing with the rest of the complex. The guesthouse was sunk into the earth so that it would barely be visible from the entry drive. The residence is glass on two sides, where sliding panels open its interior to the outside; the remaining two walls are concrete.

Guests enter the house between two board-formed concrete walls. Light, visible only in the distance, draws visitors into the earth-covered structure. Beyond an entry ramp lined with concrete columns, the building flattens and opens out to reveal the view and terrace. Inside, the concrete walls surrounding the hearth are broken away both to bring light into the space and to evoke a feeling of multiple occupations of the structure.

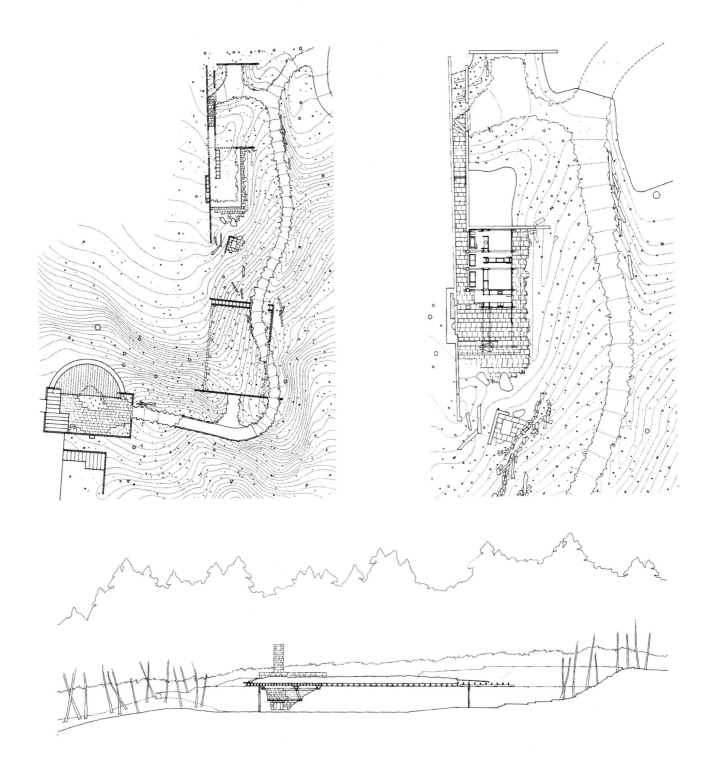

The earth-covered guesthouse
(barely visible from the entry drive)
leads visitors to the living/dining
area through a dramatic passage of
concrete columns. The progression is
a study in light and space.

Both the heavy-timber framing and trim in the guesthouse are of recycled fir. The heavy steel bracing contrasts with the fir, which both complement the rough concrete and stone used throughout the building.

Sliding panels in the dining room open to the outside, and the floor paving continues from the inside space to the outside. Massive 4 × 12-inch (102 × 305-millimeter) beams span 14 feet (4.3 meters). All came from old-growth timbers recycled from an old industrial building, which was disassembled and remilled locally.

One of the building's supporting column clusters rests on a large glacial erratic. The house is surrounded by an emergent native forest, seeded with duff lifted from a logged-over forest floor.

Garage

MEDINA, WASHINGTON

To accommodate the owners' need for a large garage for this residential compound that would not dominate the land, this vaulted structure is dug deep enough into the earth to be invisible from the drive above. The steep hillside prohibited road construction, so drivers approach the 10,000-square-foot (929-square-meter) garage by driving in front of it on a heavy wooden trestle. The trestle is supported by branching clusters of columns that resemble the big-leafed maple trees that cover the adjacent hillsides. The garage extends back into the hillside to a depth of 75 feet (22.8 meters) below grade level. Knowing that this deep an excavation would cut through several aquifers, the architects channeled the flow into a 100,000-gallon (380,000-liter) cistern that is formed by the 5-foot (1.5-meter)-deep arch restraining grade beams. The water serves for irrigation and wetland maintenance on other areas of the land.

Between the concrete arches, the vaulted roof is broken away into an interstitial space that reveals octagonal columns holding a second lid. This roof is tilted at the angle of the hillside. The pure arched forms are therefore juxtaposed with the random demands of the earth. Skylights allow light to penetrate from the rear of the building. This project is a joint venture with Peter Bohlin of Bohlin Cywinski Jackson.

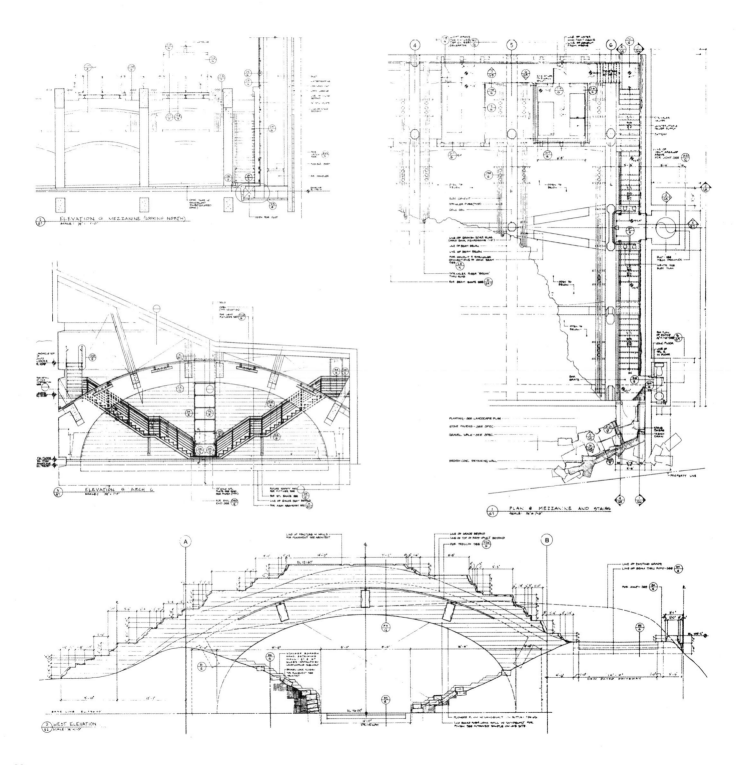

ELEVATION @ MEZZANINE (LOOKING NORTH)

ELEVATION @ ARCH 6

PLAN @ MEZZANINE AND STAIRS

WEST ELEVATION

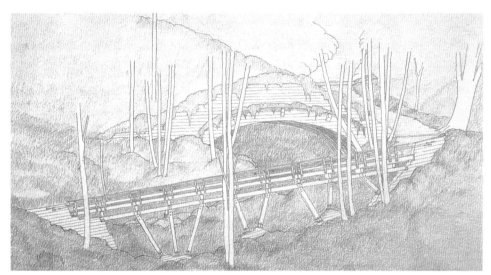

The garage holds twenty vehicles or two hundred sixty people. The arches are high enough, and the space large enough, for a women's collegiate basketball court. A key will eventually be etched into the concrete. The face of the garage is visible from the drive; skylights are the only sign from above that any structure is there at all.

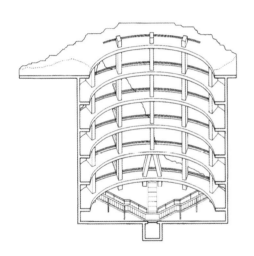

Steel braces and stairway contrast with the board-formed concrete, colored to appear weathered and warm. The octagonal columns above the arches are lit at night to reveal the true nature of the structure and the uniqueness of the earth above. Speakers are hidden in the walls of the garage, meeting the owners' requirement that technology be incorporated into the building.

Entry Turnaround

MEDINA, WASHINGTON

This covered drop-off and turnaround accommodates the many guests visiting this private residential compound. The turnaround, along a winding drive from the street, passes a guesthouse set into the steep hillside before sloping down to the entrance of the main house.

One of the challenges of the project was reconciling the linear geometry of the house with the circular geometry of the turnaround, which was dictated by the turning radius of a car. The design separates the two elements into a half-circle roof over the drop-off and a sloped plane of roof over the entry stair and then reconnects them with a covered walkway on the northern edge of the turnaround. Along the west side of the turnaround is a belvedere with views of Lake Washington, Seattle's skyline, and the Olympic Mountains in the distance.

The heavy-timber half-moon roof is set within a 30-foot (9.1-meter)-high retaining wall tucked into the hillside. Alternating sections of cedar timber stack to create the basketweave texture of the wall and a finish face for the wood shoring and steel piling that hold back the earth. A space separates the half-moon of heavy-timber roof from the retaining wall, allowing light to trickle down and illuminate the turnaround. Massive stone piers on either side of the half-circle carry a heavy-timber beam across the space, while a row of treelike columns forms a semicircle to carry the roof rafters. This project is a joint venture with Peter Bohlin of Bohlin Cywinski Jackson.

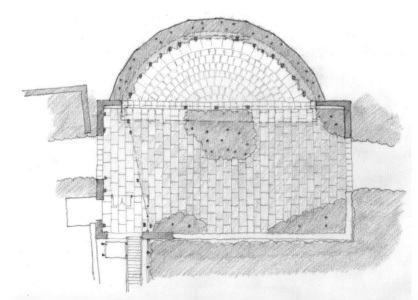

A covered walkway connects the semicircular roof over the drop-off to the sloped roof at the front door of the house.

Swimming Pool

MEDINA, WASHINGTON

Part of the large estate on the east side of Lake Washington, this swimming pool building is covered with earth and set into a hillside. Like other buildings in the complex, it integrates computer technology into a structure that is environmentally responsive. The 20 × 60-foot (6.1 × 18.3-meter) lap pool is housed in a heavy-timber building. The entire structure is fabricated from timbers recycled from dismantled industrial buildings. Wooden panels that fit into the slatted-wood walls hide high-definition video displays.

Meticulous attention was paid to details in the pool building, evident in the wood diving board, tile stairs, and stone handholds. Other features demonstrate the mix of nature and technology: glass walls open automatically to the outside; fiberglass skylights allow diffused light into the lower areas of the building; and clerestories bring in light to the higher pool space. A shower behind the large granite slab acts as the entrance to the sauna. This project is a joint venture with Peter Bohlin of Bohlin Cywinski Jackson.

The swimming pool building is made of stone and wood timbers from an old sawmill (seen at top). A smaller pool connects both the inside of the building and the outer yard, passing beneath glass panels.

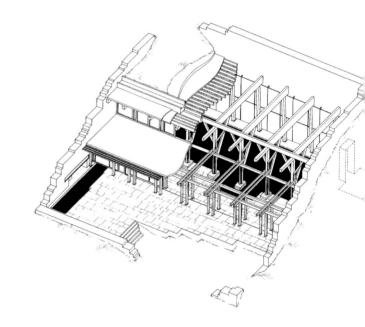

Fiberglass skylights are used to illuminate the building, since it is dug into the earth. Glass panels in the front of the building open automatically on warm days.

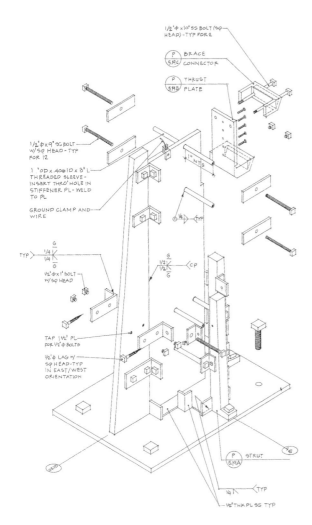

1/2" φ x 10" SS BOLT (SQ HEAD) - TYP FOR 2

⟨P⟩ BRACE
S.19C CONNECTOR

⟨P⟩ THRUST
S.19B PLATE

1/2" φ x 9" SS BOLT W/ SQ HEAD - TYP FOR 12

1 " OD x .40 ID x 3" L' THREADED SLEEVE - INSERT THRO' HOLE IN STIFFENER PL - WELD TO PL

GROUND CLAMP AND WIRE

1" NTS

TYP

G 1/4 / 1/4 G
TYP

1/2 / 1/2 G
CP

1/2" φ x 1" BOLT W/ SQ HEAD

TAP 1 1/2" PL FOR 1/2" φ BOLTS

1/2" φ LAG W/ SQ HEAD - TYP IN EAST/WEST ORIENTATION

⟨P⟩ STRUT
S.19A

6

1/4
TYP

1/2" THK PL SS TYP

Wood, stone, tile, and steel form the palette of materials for the pool building. Soaring ceilings are anchored with huge beams and highly detailed steel connectors to the stone floor. Panels slide open to reveal high-resolution video screens.

Armed Forces Memorial

NORFOLK, VIRGINIA

Letters by servicemen and women who died shortly after writing them com-memorate U.S. citizens lost in war. The architects won a national competition to design this memorial with artist Maggie Smith, who searched archives for letters from the Revolutionary War, the War of 1812, the Civil War, World Wars I and II, Korea, Vietnam, and the Persian Gulf, including one from a woman who served in the Civil War while posing as a man.

The memorial is on the most prominent point in Norfolk Harbor in Town Point Park, which runs along a pier overlooking an active industrial waterfront. To create an area for contemplation separate from the park, a bay was cut from the pier on each side of the memorial. Plank bridges cross the bays and provide a transition to the memorial plaza. Two sides of the 40-foot (3.7-meter)-square plaza open to the harbor; the landward sides are bound by low brick walls that recall fortifications built by the British on the point in the 1600s. Inscribed on the wall on either side of one bridged entry are the words of Archibald MacLeish: "We give you our deaths, give them their meaning."

The twenty bronze letters are scattered across the granite plaza as if blown in from the distant battlegrounds where U.S. citizens were killed in action. Each is three times actual size and was shaped by hand in wax before being cast in bronze. Addressed to mothers, fathers, wives, and friends, the inscriptions reveal the range of beliefs, thoughts, and emotions that form the history of the nation. Visitors bow their heads or kneel as they read in quiet reflection. Neither heroic nor monumental, the personal nature of the letters connects the living with the dead and makes their sacrifice heartfelt.

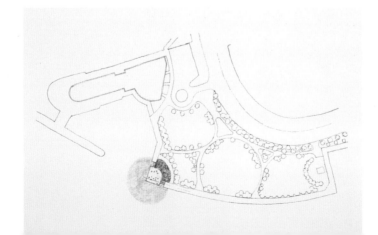

June 18, 1918

Dear Mother,

Even the trenches can be beautiful when they are trimmed with flowers, and the barbed wire forms a trellis for rambling vines, and shelter for innumerable thrushes and other songsters—one explanation, no doubt, of why the cats have a penchant for No-Man's-Land. The birds warble all the time, even when there is considerable activity, and it seems to me that their voices never sounded so sweet before. A number of them inhabit the six small trees, two birches and four wild cherry, which rise on the central island (entirely surrounded by trenches) of my strong point, or groupe de combat as the French call it. At the base of one of the birches is a flourishing wild rosebush, literally covered with blossoms, some of which I sneaked up and picked—keeping not only head but also the rest of me carefully down during the process. . . . Here are some of them for you, and also some daisies and yellow asters from the edge of one of my trenches.

Quincy Sharpe Mills
d. July 26, 1918

The memorial is on the most prominent point in Norfolk Harbor in Town Point Park, which runs along a pier overlooking an active industrial waterfront.

Wood Residence

VASHON ISLAND, WASHINGTON

A shimmer of metal roof is the first glimpse visitors get of this house along a circuitous path through the woods. The house, designed for two retired doctors, is on rural Vashon Island only a short ferry ride from Seattle. The 20-acre (8.1-hectare) property runs from forest to meadow, but the two were indistinguishable due to dense overgrowth of alder. The 2,330-square-foot (216.5-square-meter) house is a series of five pavilions that nestles along the edge of the forest to draw attention to the subtle change in the landscape.

The entry is a glazed knuckle between a public "day box" and a private "night box." The main living area is a large, open room that includes a dining area and kitchen. As with all of the pavilions, the roof over the living room starts low on the forest side and rises to a wall of windows facing the meadow on the south. A covered exterior walkway connects the pieces along the forest edge. The other pavilions contain a laundry/mud room, a greenhouse, and a garage. The wife is an avid equestrian and her husband is allergic to horses, and this arrangement allows her to shower in the laundry before she passes from a nearby stable to the house.

Throughout the house, the detailing maximizes the expressive potential of light-wood framing. Beams and columns are sandwiches of standard 2 × 8 lumber that alternate with steel knife plates. Finish materials—whether drywall or tongue-and-groove pine—stop several inches shy of the floor and ceiling to reveal the stud wall behind. They are also held back around the window openings, reducing the finishes to skins that stretch sparely over the wood skeleton beneath.

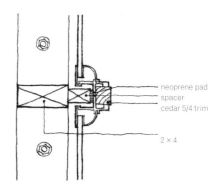

neoprene pad
spacer
cedar 5/4 trim

2 × 4

The house is a series of boxes placed to respond to the nuances of the topography and to preserve trees. Unusual details include the wood frame of the green-house, which is set on top of the wood studs.

The main living space is a large, open room with areas for entertaining, dining, and cooking. The light-wood framing both defines the space and penetrates the window wall, extending it outside.

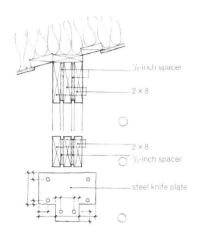

1/2-inch spacer

2 × 8

2 × 8

1/2-inch spacer

steel knife plate

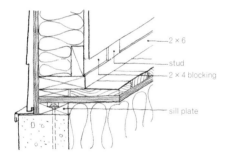

2 × 6

stud

2 × 4 blocking

sill plate

The wall finish stops several inches shy of the floor to show the wood studs. The beams are 2 × 8s that alternate with wood spacers. Steel knife plates join the beams to the columns.

Pine Forest Cabin

METHOW VALLEY, WASHINGTON

Tall and laconic like the surrounding pines, this 1,350-square-foot (125.4-square-meter) cabin has a large gable roof that gives it an iconic form. The cabin is a year-round retreat for a couple and all of their multiseason outdoor gear. The 5 acres (2 hectares) of semiarid forest is part of a vacation home development in the bucolic Methow Valley, east of the snow-tipped Cascade Mountains in north-central Washington.

The roof shelters a 16 × 65-foot (4.9 × 19.8-meter) wood platform that hovers above the steeply sloped land on seven pairs of board-formed concrete piers. Wood-framed walls, 18 feet (5.7 meters) high, run the length of the platform and are exposed at both ends of the cabin at the porches. In between, the cladding transitions from more enclosed vertical wood siding to a two-story wall of glass.

Two wood steps cantilever out from the main structure to welcome visitors to the front porch. A large overhang protects the south-facing porch from summer sun and winter snow. A glass door and a strip of high second-floor windows are the only openings that greet visitors on this wood-clad face. Inside, the long side-walls and minimal windows of the open living area create a sense of enclosure before opening to the glassed-in two-story space at the north end of the cabin. The exposed wood framing continues outside, dissolving the boundary between indoors and out, structure and trees.

The compact plan organizes built-in seating, storage, and bathrooms along the sidewalls, which frees the interior space. Upstairs is a bedroom and a loft that opens to the north-facing living space and shares its expansive views of the valley below.

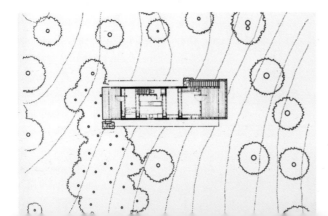

The balloon-framed walls that run the length of the platform are alternately exposed, clad in wood siding, or visible behind panes of glass. The detailing emphasizes the sense that the cabin's skin is lightly attached to the structure.

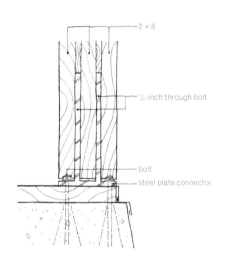

2 × 8

$1/2$-inch through bolt

bolt

steel plate connector

Steel plates connect
the triple columns to
battered concrete piers.

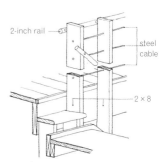

2-inch rail

steel cable

2 × 8

Layers of structure and large areas of glass foster a seamless connection between the cabin and the forest. The window wall turns the corner between the studs, underscoring the continuity of the wood framing. The exposed structure of the staircase supports the stringers and forms the guardrail.

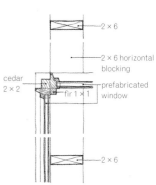

2 × 6

2 × 6 horizontal blocking

cedar 2 × 2

fir 1 × 1

prefabricated window

2 × 6

Hewitt Residence

PITTWATER, AUSTRALIA

This house, in a pocket of dense forest in a boulder-strewn valley north of Sydney, was an opportunity to work in a climate completely unlike that of the Pacific Northwest. It is one of nineteen houses that form part of an environmentally sensitive development in which over a third of the 31 acres (12.5 hectares) are held as a common nature preserve.

The geology of the area is ancient and features enormous "floater" rocks exposed by thousands of years of erosion of the surrounding sandstone. The 4,000-square-foot (371.6-square-meter) house is set in a natural clearing among large boulders on top of a hill. A bridge on axis with a large specimen gum tree cuts diagonally from a rock outcropping to a glazed entry between the main house and the library. The library is a self-contained cube set at an angle to define the entry. With 13-foot (4-meter)-high windows wrapping three sides, the space feels like a tree house set in the jungle.

The main house has two metal-wrapped cubes framing a double-height space. The north cube contains the garage on the first floor and the children's rooms above, while the south cube contains the living room and the master suite above. The kitchen, with a loftlike playroom above, straddles the central open space. Floor-to-ceiling windows and glass doors open to a large deck overlooking the jungle and distant views of the Pacific Ocean.

All exterior surfaces are metal due to the ever-present danger of fire, and the corrugated metal siding wraps the end cubes into the interior to increase the sense of continuity between inside and outside.

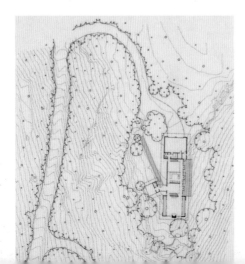

The spaces are united by an overriding corrugated metal hip roof. In the event of a bush fire, sprinklers under the eaves will wash the exterior walls with water drawn from tanks under the house. The metal materials on the exterior give way to exposed wood inside.

Schmidt Residence

SEQUIM, WASHINGTON

A beloved family cabin once stood in this clearing above Sequim Bay on the Olympic Peninsula. The land belonged to the wife's parents, and when it came back on the market, the Bay Area–based couple seized the opportunity to build their own waterfront vacation home.

The 4,500-square-foot (418-square-meter) house is split into two structures. A glazed walkway connects the main living area (with a master bedroom above) to an outbuilding containing guest rooms, a model train room, and the garage. The two wings sit perpendicularly and enclose a generous outdoor terrace, complete with fireplace, overlooking the water. The house's simple gable forms and exposed structure are set on a stone plinth and resemble a tent pitched on a platform in the woods. In some places, the stone is higher, forming fireplaces, and in others it extends out as low walls that anchor the house to the landscape or step down to the shoreline.

A long plank boardwalk through the woods to the house parallels the slope toward the water but reveals only glimpses of the bay. The front door is set perpendicular to the gable end so visitors enter under a low eave before turning into the main living area and toward an uninterrupted water view. The first floor is completely open with low cabinets, overhead beams, and a fireplace defining the kitchen, dining, and living areas. Instead of heavy-timber posts and beams, the structure features pairs of lightweight wood framing, adding to the buoyant quality of the space. The beams and columns continue beyond the glass skin of the house, dissolving the boundary between inside and outside.

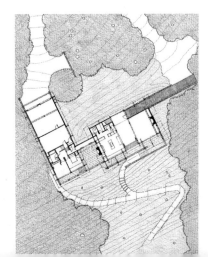

The two wings of the house, which can be closed off from each other, are joined by an outdoor terrace that overlooks the water.

The wood columns and beams continue beyond the glass panes, extending the interior space outside. The detailing of the posts and beams recalls the structural expressiveness of Japanese temple design.

Tanglefoot

PRIEST LAKE, IDAHO

Large tracts of undeveloped land harboring grizzlies, mountain caribou, and moose surround this 19-mile (30.6 kilometer)-long finger of water in northern Idaho. The owners rely on their small fleet of amphibious planes to get to this remote, 6,000-square-foot (557.4-square-meter) house on a lake. Built for the inventor who developed the birthing beds now used in most maternity wards, his wife, and their four young children, the richness of detail and structural articulation is a result of a fruitful relationship between client and architect.

To slip the house between the trees along the shoreline, it was broken into separate summer and winter blocks connected by a double-height 750-square-foot (69.7-square-meter) greenhouse that becomes a living space during mosquito season. During cold months, the summer block—with a master suite above and a conference room below—is closed, reducing the area needing heat. The balance of the living space, including the living room, kitchen, and children's bedrooms, is in the winter block.

The shingle roofs slope up, away from the view of the lake toward the woods, to capture southern light. An open catwalk passes through the light-filled double-height space along the south edge of the winter block and the greenhouse connecting the children's second-floor bedrooms to the master suite. The bedrooms are in large dormers that pop up above the roof to take in lake views on the north. They also project beyond the first floor and are held aloft by large wood brackets that define covered porches.

Wall finishes are almost entirely eliminated inside, and the exposed wood framing visible through large panes of glass blends with the tree trunks outside. Without wall finishes, though, elements typically hidden had to be rethought, leading to the use of galvanized steel conduits and industrial explosion-proof switches.

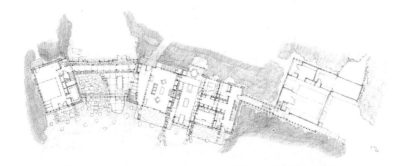

A double-height greenhouse connects the main living area in the winter block with the master suite in the summer block.

Blocks of stone pavers continue outside from the greenhouse for a seamless transition between spaces.

The kitchen is another example of rethinking industry standards. It is a room-sized stainless-steel channel holding commercial grade appliances and cabinets inserted into the wood frame of the house.

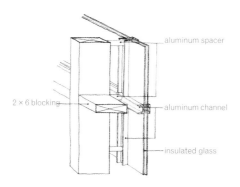

aluminum spacer

2 × 6 blocking

aluminum channel

insulated glass

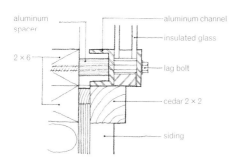

aluminum spacer

aluminum channel

insulated glass

2 × 6

lag bolt

cedar 2 × 2

siding

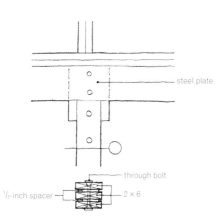

steel plate

through bolt

1/2-inch spacer

2 × 6

Aluminum spacers float a frame of aluminum channels off the face of the wood studs. The windows sit within the frame, but the tight tolerances and unusual configurations made flashing difficult until the client hunted down rolls of aluminum tape used in the aerospace industry. To accommodate Idaho's snow loads, the steel plates sandwiched between wood framing dip below the bottom of the roof beams. Galvanized freeze plugs such as those found on engine blocks cover the bolt ends.

Reeve Residence

LOPEZ ISLAND, WASHINGTON

This house creates a seamless fit between building and landscape. The pristine 120-acre (48.6-hectare) site follows a mile of convoluted shoreline, running from vertical cliffs above Puget Sound to grassy terraces with protected bays. The 2,800-square-foot (260-square-meter) house nestles discreetly amid mossy outcroppings on a bluff between forest to the north and the Strait of Juan de Fuca to the south.

As wind travels across the 30 miles (48.3 kilometers) of open water, it can whip up enough speed to shear off treetops along the cliff. To render the shed roof as inconspicuous and as streamlined as possible, it has a low pitch matching the angle of the truncated treetops. The sod-covered roof, supported by wood columns on a bluestone plinth, forms a pavilion that shelters the building's three independent volumes: a bunkhouse for children and overnight guests, a communal living area, and a master suite.

The design responds to the dual nature of this site—not only its windswept cliff side but also its more sheltering woodland side. Approaching the house from the forest, glimpses of the watery horizon are visible through the spaces between the volumes. On this face, the house presents a classically proportioned but roughly hewn wood colonnade that mimics the surrounding trees and blurs the distinction between the house and the woods.

For openness and flexibility under 250 tons of sod, the structure is outside the volumes' exterior walls. The family must travel outdoors to move between the parts of the house, but the heated stone plinth warms bare feet even in chilly weather, and the overarching roof, with its deep overhang, provides an umbrella.

The great room in the central block is a single open space with high windows that separate the white pine walls from the roof and give it the appearance of floating lightly overhead.

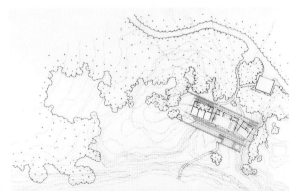

Viewed from the beach, 100 feet (30.5 meters) below, a basalt retaining wall blends into the cliff. Similarily, the wood palette of the sheltered approach fits seamlessy into the woodland.

The columns that hold up the sod roof are independent of the walls, allowing the bunkhouse and master suite to angle toward specific views.

In the great room, huge glass doors roll aside, opening up 16 feet (4.9 meters) of the south façade to the generous stone terrace. Spaces between the volumes frame coastal views. Throughout the house, the columns and structural beams combine wood studs and steel plates.

Maple Valley Library

Most of the trees that gave Maple Valley its name are gone, but this small branch library shows that building and forest can coexist. Working from arborists' detailed plans, the architects tramped through the dense understory of vine maple, salal, and fern to fine-tune their design to the land. Parking spaces slip in small clusters between tree trunks, as at a campground. In contrast to the meandering parking layout, the design of the 12,000-square-foot (1,114.8-square-meter) library (made in collaboration with Johnston Architects) is crisp and rational. Its simple, U shape allows for the most efficient use of materials and meets the modest $1.8 million budget.

The library's metal shed roof is highest along the perimeter of the building and slopes down toward a central courtyard. This minimizes the height of the library on the forest side while presenting a crown of softly glowing windows at the eave along the street. During storms, the roof funnels rainwater to a downspout that pours into a sculptural pool in the courtyard. This dramatic display is both poetic and functional, demonstrating the runoff urban development creates while filtering stormwater through the gravel bottom of the pool.

From a porch, visitors enter directly into the main reading room. Its scale and proportions, 50 × 140 feet (15.2 × 42.7 meters), give it the stateliness of a classic Carnegie library reading room. Its power lies in the expressiveness of the exposed structure. The children's reading area in the north corner looks onto large firs and ancient stumps; the adults' area on the south overlooks a cluster of vine maples. At night, the large wood-framed windows at once forge a strong connection to the trees outside and convey a welcoming civic presence.

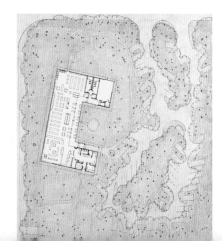

A 3-foot (0.9-meter)-high concrete wall provides a solid base from which the wood stud walls rise from the forest floor. The rustic surface makes the library look like it was built on the foundation of an old, abandoned building reclaimed by the forest.

A rhythm of exposed 2 × 6 wood studs circles the room. Window frames are fixed to the outside of the frame so the floor-to-ceiling wood studs are visible through the glass, blurring the boundary between interior and exterior.

153

Grace Episcopal Church

BAINBRIDGE ISLAND, WASHINGTON

For years, the parishioners of this Episcopalian church worshipped in a basement before buying 12 acres (4.9 hectares) of land on Bainbridge Island that had been clear-cut a decade earlier and was overgrown with scotch broom and alder trees. Now the transition from the secular to the spiritual begins with a view from a gravel drive all the way through the sanctuary to a big leaf maple on a hillside. A 100-foot (30.5-meter)-diameter circle filled with alder trees is ringed by parking, eliminating the asphalt lot that typically greets parishioners. A path through the center of the circle aligns with the sanctuary and the maple tree beyond. Over time, the congregation will watch the woods grow up again around the church.

A glacial stone, green-gray with flecks of red, found on the land, stands out-side the church. Honed on the top and back but otherwise left rough, it is now the baptismal font. A zinc strip that delivers water to the font runs down the side of the stone to a cross at the terminus of the sanctuary.

The church is minimalist in its materials—wood and concrete—but it has a Gothic richness and scale that comes from its structure and details. Pairs of 24-foot (7.3-meter)-tall battered piers of concrete frame the narthex and the sanctuary and provide lateral stability in the otherwise open sanctuary. A king post truss runs between the piers and carries the sanctuary roof on its upper chord. Its lower chord supports the edge of the low roof over the side aisles. The rafters over the side aisles continue into the sanctuary in a filigree of wood that modulates the scale of the 35-foot (10.7-meter)-tall sanctuary.

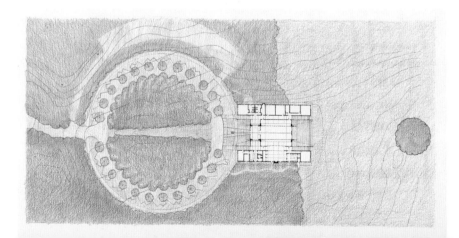

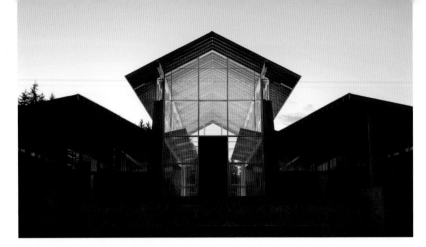

Parishioners pass through a forecourt defined by the two wings of the church. To the east are classrooms, to the west are social spaces and offices. The wings also define an outdoor terrace on the south side of the sanctuary for gatherings after services. A stone memorial wall for interning ashes steps down toward the woods and the maple.

Detailing throughout the church is meticulous, creating an environment that is both rich and serene.

Like tracery, steel rods cross in front of the clerestory windows between the side aisle and sanctuary roof; the space is infused with natural light.

Capitol Hill Library

SEATTLE, WASHINGTON

This branch library, designed with Johnston Architects, provides a place of refuge in Seattle's most densely populated urban neighborhood. It replaces an undersized 1954 library on this small corner lot, a block away from the main shopping street.

The new 11,615-square-foot (1,079-square-meter) library is almost a perfect square in plan. A V-shaped opening slices through the two-story building at the angle of the sun at winter solstice and defines a double-height reading room with a wall of windows on the south elevation. A large triangle of metal roof covers the reading room, beginning over a reading porch outside the large south-facing windows, and slopes to a point 38 feet (11.6 meters) above the sidewalk over a prow of trellis that marks the main entrance on the north.

The bricks were tumbled to age them so they would fit with the historic brick apartment building to the south. The mortar was trowel struck to give the walls a monolithic quality. A metal trellis planted with nineteen varieties of vine is held off the wall on short aluminum legs and is interrupted by a large bay window containing reading nooks. The trellis wraps the brick walls and continues the green wall inside the library.

At the street intersection, a two-story window turns the corner and resembles a book-filled lantern. A ramp leads up from the corner to the midblock entry within the triangular trellis. Inside is a double-height reading room framed by administration spaces, meeting rooms, and offices. Library patrons pass under a bridge, which links a community meeting room to a neighborhood service center on the second-floor mezzanine, and into the generous light-filled space.

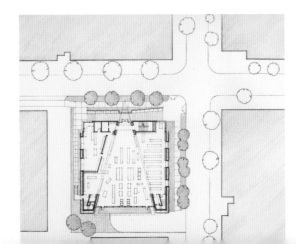

Lighting by artist Iole Aessandrini will make the ivy-covered entrance glow at night.

A trellis wraps around the brick walls and into the library to create a vertical garden.

Large bay windows contain reading nooks along the street. At the entrance, the ivy-covered trellis will screen benches from passers-by.

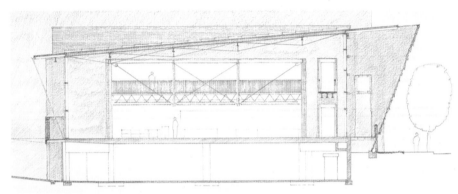

The triangular metal prow of trellis signals the main entrance.

The ivy-covered trellis continues inside the library and will cover the brick walls in a blanket of green. A thin strip of skylight seperates the wedge of sloped roof from the brick walls and appears to float overhead.

The library provides an oasis in one of Seattle's densest urban neighborhoods.

Long Residence

ORCAS ISLAND, WASHINGTON

This retreat on Orcas Island along the Harney Channel has a view of the green and white Washington State ferries as they ply their watery route among the San Juan Islands. The house sits on a shallow south-facing strip of land along the narrow waterway. Because there is little fetch (the amount of open space on water where wind builds up), the roof can pitch up toward the water without fear of a gale ripping it off.

The design of the house, which is all about supporting the roof, also provided an opportunity to underscore the raw beauty and power of trees in their more natural state. Western red cedars were harvested from the contractor's father's land and then water-blasted to remove the bark and reveal their skeletal form. The six logs, between 12 and 60 feet (3.7 and 18.3 meters) long, are hoisted in the air on bundled tripods of cedar poles.

The logs and beams sit on a simple rectilinear concrete platform that retains earth on the north side of the house and forms a large terrace on the south, where the steep hillside slopes down to the water. The longest log runs parallel to the north wall of the house along the forest and supports the low edge of the roof as it slopes upward to 15 feet (4.6 meters). Three logs sit at a slight angle to each other along the south to form a segmented arch that captures a view of the channel. A glass wall with large panes and few mullions sits outside the structure, wrapping it on three sides.

Visitors arrive through the woods along the north edge of the house, which is nestled into the forest floor. A series of small windows in the otherwise opaque wood-shingled façade frames vignettes of the wood tripods inside.

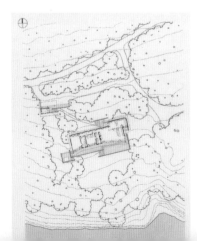

A glass skin wraps a skeletal structure of peeled cedar logs held aloft on bundled log tripods.

The entry is into a low enclosed area on the north that widens as the ceiling slopes up over the main living and dining area toward the channel. The wood tripods resist lateral loads and express structural stability.

The peeled cedar logs inside underscore the beauty and power of the trees outside.

A New Joint Port of Entry

OROVILLE, WASHINGTON, AND OSOYOOS, BRITISH COLUMBIA

This border crossing between the United States and Canada is one of the first new shared facilities built since the enactment of the Joint Border Accord of 1995. The only port of entry in the region, it serves a major arterial highway between eastern Washington and British Columbia. Due to its important location, it provides twenty-four-hour service for both noncommercial and commercial vehicles and processes high-risk cargo.

The crossing is near Lake Osoyoos in the fertile Okanogan Valley, home of some of the finest and most productive fruit orchards in North America. The design employs Lombardy poplars to orient travelers and provide visual cues about how to proceed. As cars approach, a row of columnar trees is visible over the surrounding orchards, signaling that the border is near. The road passes through these trees and into an open zone between the first row of trees and another planted along the border. Cars then turn and move parallel to the border to reach the customs booths. The parallel walls of poplars focus the views toward the Cascade Mountain range (for those crossing into Canada) and the lake (for those coming into the United States). Drivers turn once more and pass through a third row of trees, marking the end of the process.

The 918-foot (280-meter)-long port building straddles the border. Programmatic requirements differ between the two countries, but a shed roof runs the length of the building to unify disparate elements. Below, traffic lanes and inspection booths separate the U.S. and Canadian administration and multipurpose buildings—one-story bars perpendicular to and penetrating the long building.

The first-floor walls are simple tilt-up concrete panels; however, the design features modulated panel sizes, extensive windows, and expressive steel connection details. The walls sit inboard of an exposed steel structure supporting the shed roof. The plus-shaped steel columns have four flanges that allow the building to be physically erected with bolts instead of welding.

Approaching drivers pass under a continuous shed roof that covers the inspection booths and connects the U.S. and Canadian administration buildings. A section of the shed roof is cut at the border and infilled with glass to identify this significant but otherwise invisible line.

The economical but refined structure combines tilt-up concrete
panels, like those of the local
fruit warehouses, with exposed
steel columns and beams.

Flint Beach Residence

LOPEZ ISLAND, WASHINGTON

This 2,600-square-foot (241.5-square-meter) guesthouse sits on the same 120-acre (48.6-hectare) private preserve above Puget Sound as the Reeve Residence and was built for the same family. Sheltered within the quiet of the forest above a protected inlet, the house provides the family with both greater autonomy when visiting the island and easy access to the beach for kayaking.

The topography of the site informs the design of the residence, which was fabricated as three independent volumes that follow the contours of the bay below. To further emphasize the connection to place, the entry axis along a wood colonnade focuses on a single weathered tree growing on a tombolo, a rocky islet linked to the main island by a spit of sand.

To the east, past the cedar-shingled garage, the first element houses the entry and living room. The center element contains the kitchen and dining room and the westernmost the bedrooms and a den. Each volume is angled southwest toward the bay, an orientation reinforced by the slope of the deep-eaved metal shed roofs.

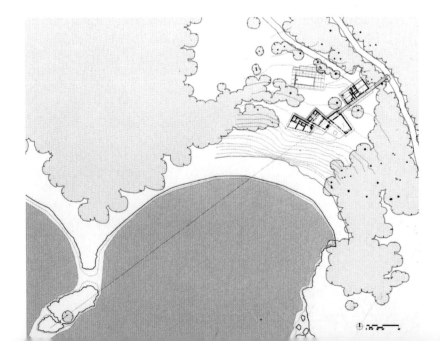

Forming one side of the covered walkway that leads to the entry with its view of the bay is a fourth volume that houses a garage and extra guest quarters above.

The staggered volumes accommodate bluestone terraces that overlook the inlet. The outdoor fireplace of the first terrace is a darkened galvanized steel plate. The kitchen entry on the forest side leads to a pool area to the north.

Exposed 2 × 4 and 2 × 6 walls are designed and braced to emphasize the forces and loads inherent in light framing. Throughout, fenestration is carefully considered to capture light and views.

Mallorca Residence

PUERTO ANDRATX, MALLORCA, SPAIN

Mallorca is Spain's largest island and a popular tourist destination. To the south-west lies Puerto Andratx, with its small fishing port and large leisure harbor. Set on the eastern shore of the natural harbor, this 4,900-square-foot (455.2-square-meter) residence was designed around the shells of two existing buildings. Connecting the two structures is large a central courtyard that focuses attention northwest toward the Mediterranean Sea and ties the whole residence to the rugged landscape.

For the main living areas that face each other across the courtyard, the architects took advantage of the mild climate. The long glass walls fold back, opening the interior to the outdoors and creating one flowing space with the courtyard and adjacent covered porches. An enclosed parking court buffers the house from the street. Visitors enter the residence down a staircase and through tall screens, symmetrically on axis with the pine-shaded courtyard. From inside, a narrow opening above the entrance reveals glimpses of the massive palm tree that defines the other end of this axis.

Great care was taken to preserve existing vegetation and to fit the building well into its context. Throughout is a palette of materials native to Spain. Stuccoed concrete-block walls and wooden roofs sheathed with clay tiles order the structure. Stones for walls and piers were quarried locally. The matting used for fencing and screening is *brezo*, another local material.

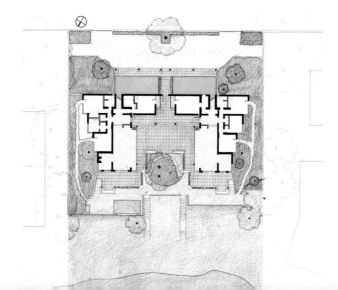

The design allows for over 2,000 square feet (185.8 square meters) of terraces that extend the living spaces outdoors.

To either side of the main courtyard, stairs leads down to the pool level with its cluster of pines; below, a path steps down to the rocky shore.

In contrast to the rugged surfaces outside, the materials of the interior are polished. Floors and fireplaces are laid with Mallorcan marble quarried several miles from the harbor.

Studio and Guesthouse at Meteor Vineyards

NAPA, CALIFORNIA

Set among 27 acres (10.9 hectares) of vineyards, meadows, and oak groves in Napa Valley, this studio and guesthouse each terminate an axis of the main residence. Their individual designs respond to distinctive aspects of the land.

The 360-square-foot (33.4-square-meter) studio is a smaller version of the main house, with its rammed-earth walls and metal roof. The battered 30-inch (762-millimeter)-thick walls define an L-shaped enclosure among a grove of eighty-year-old oaks. One wall parallels the trellised walkway from the main house that terminates in a small outdoor pool in the crook of the L. The roof of the studio slopes back to this corner; during rainstorms, water pours into the pool. The entry is between the pool and a plywood-clad bathroom; otherwise, the studio is a single open space with glass walls offering views of the gnarled trees.

Visitors follow a bridge from the main house to reach the 1,200-square-foot (111.5-square-meter) guesthouse that hovers over the vines. A narrow opening in the rammed-earth walls leads to an exterior, covered passageway that cuts through the center of the guesthouse to an outdoor terrace and pool on the west, with views of the rolling hills. A V-shaped wing of metal roof floats above the massive walls on exposed wood framing and funnels rainwater into the pool. A shared living and dining area is on the north side, where the rammed-earth wall steps down to reveal a wood-framed glass wall. To the south, across the covered passageway, are three bedroom suites. A pair of French doors opens each room to the vineyard with a small balcony the depth of the rammed earth. Clerestory windows bring light inside between the top of the wall and the slope of the roof above.

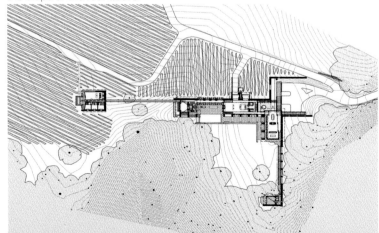

A variety of soils from the surrounding hills create marbled layers in the rammed-earth walls.

The design of the studio allows for both privacy and openness.

French doors punctuate the guest-house's rammed-earth wall at each of the three private suites.

The guest suites share an open living and dining area with views of the vineyard. The axis from the main house terminates in a pool.

Main Residence
at Meteor Vineyards

NAPA, CALIFORNIA

The 12,316-square-foot (114-square meter) residence on a tree-studded hillside immerses the family in the distinctive landscape of this wine-growing region, where stellar vintages depend on a harmony of climate and earth. The L-shaped main house encloses an edge of a meadow that is otherwise bounded by oak groves. One axis extends along a 124-foot (37.8-meter) walkway south to the studio. The other axis follows a 130-foot (39.6-meter) bridge westward to the guesthouse in the vineyards.

The house is constructed of thick rammed-earth walls along the vineyard and rammed-earth piers, light wood framing, and glass on its more private aspect. The butterfly roofs were designed to catch the valley's limited rainfall for irrigation around the residence.

The clients requested a house that would not only fit into the landscape, but also provide generous spaces for entertaining and raising their family. The main wing comprises a family room and an informal dining, with the kitchen in the crook of the L. The east wing that extends toward the studio houses the formal dining room and living room. On the second floor, the master suite overlooks the pool terrace and shares a chimney with the outdoor fireplace. The bedroom block also includes a library, a play area, and the children's rooms. The plan allows for some flexibility as to assignment of rooms as the kids become older.

A breezeway connector by the pool leads past the spa and exercise room toward the guesthouse. The pool and terraces above open onto the meadow, which serves as an observable area where the children can play.

A fairly open plan delineated with low partitions and a myriad of windows enhances the substantial mass of the structure. Below ground, an extensive wine cellar and tasting room of rammed earth lack windows but seem to glow from within.

Orlean Gillespie Residence

GALLATIN, NEW YORK

Surrounding this 2,700-square-foot (250.8-square-meter) Hudson Valley residence is a collage of rolling hills, pasture land, and encroaching forest. Stone fences that bound the fields and run through the fifty-year-old woodland tell something of the complex history of the region. To reveal the poignancy of this landscape determined the organization of the house.

Winding through a stand of black locust trees, the driveway arrives at a small parking area. Two stone walls border a narrow walk through the trees to the entrance. Here, a stone-walled entry reinforces the experience of compression. To step into the main living spaces is to be released into a 180-degree view that sweeps across meadowland to the Taconic range in the distance. The roof further dramatizes the vista by pitching up to allow floor-to-ceiling windows.

The plan is organized into a public block comprising the kitchen, living, and dining areas and a semiprivate block containing a study and bedrooms. The more open public block is framed with a glulaminated post-and-beam structure while the private block is stud-wall construction, except for the side of the study that faces a courtyard, where it repeats the glulaminated structure. The small south-facing courtyard that separates the two blocks allows the owners to live outside in the cooler fall and spring months.

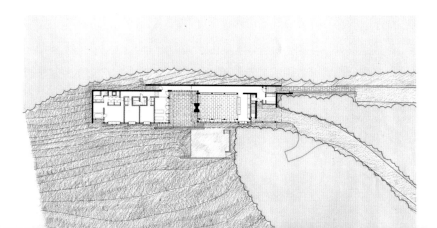

The interplay of mottled stone entry and windows that run the length of the house is one of compression and expansion. A meadow slopes gently away to the south.

A small lawn complements the wilder woods and meadow. An outdoor fireplace further enhances the livability of the courtyard.

A long open corridor joins the public and private blocks. The main living space has low built-in storage and window seats that barely interrupt the wall of glass.

In the spalike bathroom, the planes of mirrors, walls, windows, and lights create a constantly unfolding sense of space. A soaking tub in the corner takes in the sweeping view.

Ohana House at Niulii

NORTH KOHALA, ISLAND OF HAWAII, HAWAII

Trade winds blow across the northern coast of the Island of Hawaii unrelentingly, bringing with them intermittent rainsqualls and variable sunshine. A mile inland atop a blustery hillside, this 2,600-square-foot (241.5-square-meter) house occupies one parcel of a 75-acre (30.4-hectare) estate where, for over a century, sugar cane was farmed. The owners spent years cleaning up the land, which now lies within a protected conservation zone, and are letting it return to native grasses and tropical trees like the hala.

Every aspect of the plan, form, and materials was shaped by the circumstances of wind, sun, and topography. To frame panoramic views of the Pacific while also sheltering a series of outdoor living spaces, three distinct volumes were organized in a U around a south-facing courtyard. The central box to the north encompasses the kitchen, dining, and living rooms and is completely glazed so that the ocean is visible through the kitchen from the courtyard. The box to the east contains the bedrooms and that to the west houses a garage, laundry, and media room. This arrangement creates two oceanfront terraces at the outer corners. The northeast terrace extends the living room outside on calm days. The northwest terrace provides a wind-buffered spot for alfresco dining with views of the sunset and distant Maui.

The shedlike shape of the house takes its cue from the prevailing winds. The roofs tilt down toward the wind at the angle of the hill below. To insure structural integrity even in sustained gales, the building is anchored to the earth. Steel plates attached to the window mullions pin into the stone foundation and lace into the rafters.

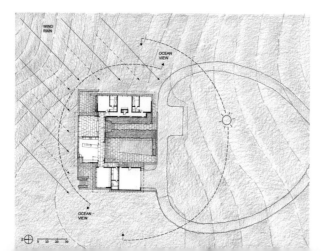

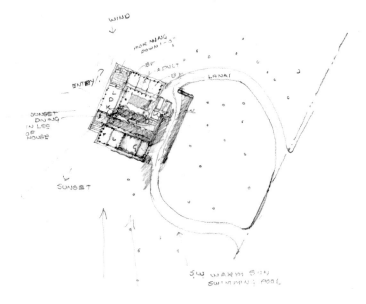

Cedar-shingled walls rise from a massive rock base of 'a'a, a local lava. The pitch of the roofs reflects the angle of the trade winds, which constantly blow between 10 and 40 knots per hour.

The sun-warmed pool court is planted with bamboo and alahe'e, a native shrub whose flowers are used for making leis. Enormous rolling glass doors extend the space across the interior. The blurring of indoors and out is further reinforced by the basalt stone flooring that covers both the courtyard and the main corridor.

Using steel ties that run through wood columns or attach to window mullions (see detail on page 237), then cross brace between posts, allows the structure to remain open and light.

One end of the south corridor spills into the media room; the other leads to the bedrooms for family and guests (*'ohana*, after all, means "extended family"). The cabinetry and millwork throughout the interior are eucalyptus wood.

Spring Creek Ranch
Golf House

COLLERVILLE, TENNESSEE

Once a functioning cattle ranch, this golf club in Western Tennessee sets a
Jack Nicklaus–designed golf course within a pastoral landscape of wetlands,
woodlands, and wildflower meadows. The 23,704-square-foot (2,202.2-square-
meter) Golf House leads visitors between narrow stone walls and along opaque
passages to more strongly emphasize the power of the views onto the surrounding course, trees, and lakes.

The plan distributes activities along three distinct pavilions: to the east, the
pro shop and administration offices, with exercise rooms below; along the north-
south axis, the men's and women's locker rooms, with cart storage below; and to
the west, the dining rooms and lounge.

The roof of the pro shop pavilion, like that of the gatehouse, is fabricated with
simple span rafters supported by wood columns and concrete piers. By contrast,
the dining and locker pavilions feature 50-foot (15.2-meter)-long glulaminated
and steel trusses that span between concrete piers. The trusses carry a wooden
roof structure, inset with a narrow strip of glazing at the apex. All solid partitioning stops 8 feet (2.4 meters) above the floor and all acoustical closures are
executed in glass. Thus the structure itself, and the physics of gravity, becomes
the dominant element of the design.

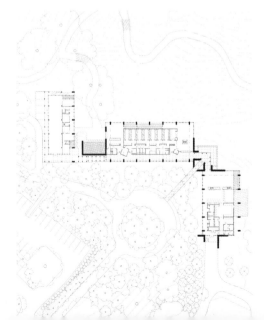

A driveway sweeps under the deep eaves of the pro shop and administration pavilion where members check in; from here they can move along a covered walkway to the locker pavilion or head to the practice range and queue for the first tee. For those coming just to dine, a walkway off the circular drive ushers members into the embrace of two stone walls at the foyer.

The locally quarried stone elements, used as extended partitioning and as fireplace surrounds, are nonstructural.

Purchase, New York, Residence

WESTCHESTER COUNTY, NEW YORK

The rolling forested terrain of Westchester County, part of the New York Metropolitan Area, has been heavily developed with small towns and suburbs and is criss-crossed by highways and roads. The 10,000-square-foot (929-square-meter) Purchase Residence is designed to surround the family with both the remaining natural woodland and meticulously landscaped outdoor spaces while muting the noise of a nearby interstate.

A four-courtyard scheme organizes the residence into five zones. The central pavilion, which houses the living and dining areas, the kitchen, and a family room, is reached either by the formal guest entrance to the east or up a similarly formal entrance on axis to the west. The entire volume is glazed for unobstructed views onto the courtyards. Bedrooms are ordered along a wing to the southwest; the wife's office, den, and guest room are clustered in a wing at the northwest corner. Bay windows pierce the public façade of each of these pavilions for controlled views. Across the courtyards are a wing with a gymnasium and a library and a separate pavilion for the husband's office.

The distribution of spaces and the treatment of materials reflects the relative formality of the culture and architecture of this affluent suburb. One such instance can be found in the bluestone walls that enclose the residence: Laid with roughened faces on the exterior, the walls are polished smooth as they turn inward to become a central element of the interior.

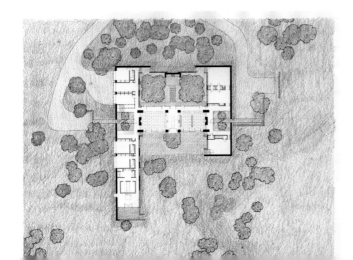

The interplay of openings and enclosures serves to protect the owners' privacy while introducing light and views. The small terrace off the master suite shows the varying effects of the bluestone's treatment.

The courtyards open the residence onto a strictly ordered landscape.

A subdued palette of materials contrasts the cool blue-gray of the stonework with the warm tones of the fir framing and riftsawn red oak millwork.

DETAILS, FURNITURE, AND HARDWARE

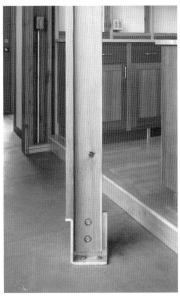

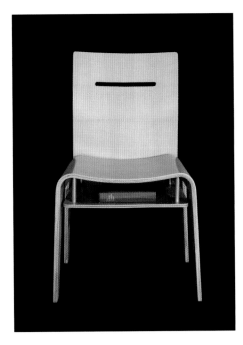

GRACE CHAIR

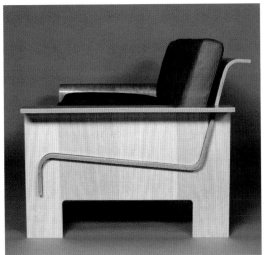

HANNAH COUCH

PUGET PULL

ANDERSON PULL

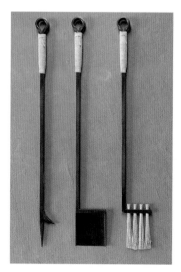

ORLEAN GILLESPIE FIREPLACE TOOLS

DOOR KNOCKER

SWITCH PLATE

MERCER LEVER

CYPRESS LEVER

ORCAS LEVER

CUTLER LEVER

BAINBRIDGE LEVER

BAINBRIDGE LEVER STAINLESS

CREDITS.

PARKER RESIDENCE,
Bainbridge Island, Washington, 1984

Client: Jim and Lucille Parker
Project Team: Jim Cutler, Amy Hiatt
Contractor: Colegrove Brothers Construction
Photographer: Art Grice
AIA NATIONAL HONOR AWARD, 1986
AIA SEATTLE HONOR AWARD, 1985
AIA/WESTERN RED CEDAR ASSOCIATION FIRST AWARD, 1985
AIA/SUNSET/WESTERN HOME AWARD MERIT AWARD, 1984

THE BRIDGE HOUSE,
Bainbridge Island, Washington, 1987

Client: Gale Cool
Project Team: Jim Cutler, Jeff Garlid
Contractor: James McDonald Kennedy
Structural Engineer: Greg Hiatt
Photographers: Peter Aaron/Esto (pp. 21, 24 middle, 25),
Art Grice (pp. 20, 23, 24 bottom), Jim Cutler (p. 24 top)
AIA/WOOD COUNCIL MERIT AWARD, 1989
AIA/WESTERN RED CEDAR ASSOCIATION MERIT AWARD, 1989
AIA/SUNSET/WESTERN HOME AWARD CITATION, 1991
SEATTLE TIMES/AIA HOME OF THE YEAR HONOR AWARD, 1988

WRIGHT GUESTHOUSE,
The Highlands, Washington, 1987

Client: Bagely and Virginia Wright
Project Team: Jim Cutler, Bruce Anderson,
Amy Hiatt
Contractor: Charter Construction
Structural Engineer: Greg Hiatt
Photographers: Peter Aaron/Esto (pp. 26, 27, 29 top,
32–34, 35 top), Art Grice (pp. 29 middle, bottom, 35 middle,
bottom), Langdon Clay (pp. 30, 31)
AIA SEATTLE HONOR AWARD, 1988
AIA/WOOD COUNCIL MERIT AWARD, 1988

VIRGINIA MERRILL BLOEDEL
EDUCATION CENTER,
Bloedel Reserve, Bainbridge Island,
Washington, 1992

Client: Prentice Bloedel
Project Team: Jim Cutler, David Cinamon, Bruce
Anderson, Nick Reid
Contractor: Charter Construction
Structural Engineer: Dave Eisenman, KPFF Consulting
Engineers
Photographers: Chris Eden (p. 46), Richard Brown (p. 39
bottom), Art Grice (pp. 36, 37, 39 top, 40–45, 47 middle,
bottom), Cutler Anderson Architects (p. 47 top)
AIA NATIONAL HONOR AWARD, 1993
AIA NORTHWEST REGIONAL AWARD, 1994
AIA SEATTLE HONOR AWARD, 1992
AIA/WOOD COUNCIL HONOR AWARD, 1992

SALEM WITCH TRIALS
TERCENTARY MEMORIAL,
Salem, Masachusetts, 1992
(IN COLLABORATION WITH MAGGIE SMITH, ARTIST)

Client: The City of Salem
Project Team: Jim Cutler, Maggie Smith,
Bruce Anderson, David Cinamon
Contractor: Hayden Hillsgrove
Landscape Architect: Cynthia Smith and
Craig Halvorsen, Halvorsen & Associates
Photographers: ©1992 Steve Rosenthal (pp. 49–53),
Maggie Smith (p. 48)
Model Photographer: Paul Lyden (p. 51)
AIA NATIONAL HONOR AWARD, 1994
AIA SEATTLE HONOR AWARD, 1993
BOSTON SOCIETY OF ARCHITECTS
HONOR AWARD, 1993

PAULK RESIDENCE,
Seabeck, Washington, 1994

Client: Elinor and John Paulk
Project Team: Jim Cutler, Bruce Anderson
Contractor: Pleasant Beach Construction
Structural Engineer: Ratti Swenson Perbix
Photographers: Art Grice (pp. 54, 55, 57 top, 58–61, 62 middle, bottom, 63, 65), Timothy Hursley, reprinted by permission from *House Beautiful*, © July 1996, The Hearst Corporation. All rights reserved (pp. 57 bottom, 62 top, 64).
   AIA SEATTLE HONOR AWARD, 1994
   AIA/WOOD COUNCIL MERIT AWARD, 1995
   AIA/WESTERN RED CEDAR EXCELLENCE AWARD, 1994
   AIA/SUNSET/WESTERN HOME AWARD CITATION, 1995

GUESTHOUSE,
Medina, Washington, 1993
(JOINT VENTURE WITH BOHLIN CYWINSKI JACKSON)

Client: Private
Project Team: Jim Cutler, Pat Munter, Bruce Anderson; from BCJ: Peter Bohlin, Theresa Thomas, Russ Hamlet, Robert Miller
Contractor: Sellen Construction Co.
Landscape Architect: The Berger Partnership
Structural Engineer: KPFF Consulting Engineers
Mechanical/Electrical Engineer: Interface Engineering
Photographers: Karl Backus (pp. 67, 69 middle, 70 bottom, 72, 73, 76 top, bottom, 77), Art Grice (pp. 66, 69 top, bottom, 70 top, middle, 71, 74, 75, 76 middle)

GARAGE,
Medina, Washington, 1992
(JOINT VENTURE WITH BOHLIN CYWINSKI JACKSON)

Client: Private
Project Team: Jim Cutler, Pat Munter, Bruce Anderson, Dave Cinamon, Lydia Marshall, Nick Reid; from BCJ: Peter Bohlin, Terrence Wagner, Robert Miller, Don Maxwell
Contractor: Sellen Construction Co.
Landscape Architect: The Berger Partnership
Structural Engineer: KPFF Consulting Engineers
Mechanical/Electrical Engineer: Interface Engineering
Photographers: Chris Eden (pp. 79, 81 bottom, 82, 83), Art Grice (p. 81 top), Pat Munter (p. 78)

ENTRY TURNAROUND,
Medina, Washington, 1995
(JOINT VENTURE WITH BOHLIN CYWINSKI JACKSON)

Client: Private
Project Team: Jim Cutler, Bruce Anderson, Pat Munter, Mark Wettstone; from BCJ: Peter Bohlin, Terrence Wagner, Robert Miller, Bill Loose
Landscape Architect: The Berger Partnership
Structural Engineer: KPFF Consulting Engineers
Contractor: Sellen Construction Company
Photographers: Art Grice, Jim Cutler, Bruce Anderson, Karl Backus

SWIMMING POOL,
Medina, Washington, 1995
(JOINT VENTURE WITH BOHLIN CYWINSKI JACKSON)

Client: Private
Project Team: Jim Cutler, Pat Munter, Bruce Anderson, Stephen Rising; from BCJ: Peter Bohlin, Bill Loose, Shane Chandler
Contractor: Sellen Construction Co.
Landscape Architect: The Berger Partnership
Structural Engineer: KPFF Consulting Engineers
Mechanical/Electrical Engineer: Interface Engineering
Photographers: Art Grice (pp. 90, 91, 93 middle, bottom, 94–97), Lydia Marshall (p. 93 top)

ARMED FORCES MEMORIAL,
Norfolk, Virginia, 1998
(IN COLLABORATION WITH MAGGIE SMITH, ARTIST)

Client: City of Norfolk
Project Team: Jim Cutler, Lee Braun, Maggie Smith
Landscape Architect: Verdigris Landscape Architects
Engineers: URS Consultants, MMM Design Group, Mark Anderson at Walla Walla Foundry
Contractor: Techon
Photographers: John Wadsworth (pp. 99, 100 bottom), Jim Cutler (pp. 100 top, 101)

WOOD RESIDENCE,
Vashon Island, Washington, 1998

Client: Barbara Wood and Bill Schlaer
Project Team: Jim Cutler, David Cinamon,
George Houdek
Landscape Architect: Verdigris Landscape Architects
Contractor: Pete Crocker
Photographers: Art Grice, Undine Prohl

PINE FOREST CABIN,
Methow Valley, Washington, 1999

Client: Private
Project Team: Jim Cutler, Bruce Anderson, Russ Hamlet,
Joe Hurley, David Cinamon
Structural Engineer: Monte Clark Engineering
Contractor: Bjornsen Construction
Photographer: Art Grice
  AIA NATIONAL HONOR AWARD, 2000
  AIA NORTHWEST & PACIFIC REGION
    MERIT AWARD, 2001
  WOOD DESIGN MERIT AWARD, 2001
  AIA SEATTLE HONOR AWARD, 2000

HEWITT RESIDENCE,
Pittwater, Australia, 2000

Client: Jonathan Hewitt
Project Team: Jim Cutler, David Wagner
Structural Engineer: Greg Hiatt
Photographer: Anthony Browell at
Oki Doki Words & Pictures

SCHMIDT RESIDENCE,
Sequim, Washington, 2000

Client: Ron and Lila Schmidt
Project Team: Jim Cutler, David Wagner
Stone Mason: Tony Rodhiger
Contractor: Alford Homes
Photographers: Art Grice (pp. 121–23, 125),
John Granen (p. 124)
  AIA/SUNSET/WESTERN HOME MERIT AWARD, 2001

TANGLEFOOT,
Priest Lake, Idaho, 2001

Client: Private
Project Team: Jim Cutler, Lee Braun, David Wagner
Structural Engineer: Craig Lee at Coffman Engineers
Contractor: Owner and Humble Homes
Photographer: Art Grice

REEVE RESIDENCE,
Lopez Island, Washington, 2001

Client: Tom and Sally Reeve
Project Team: Jim Cutler, Janet Longenecker, Julie Cripe
Structural Engineer: DeAnn Arnholtz at Coffman
Engineers
Stone Mason: Tony Rodhiger
Cabinets: Dan Nichols
Interior Design: Susan Okamoto
Contractor: Russet Construction
Head Framer: Brett Ackerman
Photographer: Art Grice
  AIA/SUNSET/WESTERN HOME MERIT AWARD, 2003–04
  AIA SEATTLE HONOR AWARD, 2002
  WOOD DESIGN HONOR AWARD, 2002

MAPLE VALLEY LIBRARY,
Maple Valley, Washington, 2001
(IN COLLABORATION WITH JOHNSTON ARCHITECTS)

Client: King County Library System
Project Team: Jim Cutler, Ray Johnston of Johnston
Architects, Marc Peveto, David Cinamon
Structural Engineer: Swenson Say Faget
M/E/P Engineers: SvR Engineers
Arborist: Jim Barbarinis
Roofing Consultant: Ray Wetherholt
Landscape Architect: Swift & Company
Lighting Designer: Patrick Tilley at McGowan Broz
Engineers
Interior Design: Nancy Burfiend, NB Design
Contractor: R. Miller Commercial Contractors, Lonnie
Crabtree, Construction Manager
Photographer: Art Grice
  AIA NATIONAL HONOR AWARD, 2001
  BUILDING WITH TREES AWARD OF EXCELLENCE, 2003
  AIA SEATTLE HONOR AWARD, 2001
  WOOD DESIGN HONOR AWARD, 2001

GRACE EPISCOPAL CHURCH,
Bainbridge Island, Washington, 2003

Client: Diocese of Olympia and Grace Episcopal Church
Congregation
Project Team: Jim Cutler, Bruce Anderson,
Pat Munter, Chad Harding, Hiroki Kurozumi,
Garrett Naylor
Structural Engineer: Greg Hiatt
Civil Engineer: David Browne
Acoustical Engineer: Michael R. Yantis Associates
Contractor: Drury Construction Company, Marty Sievertson, Project Manager, and Mike Patterson, Superintendent
Photographer: Art Grice
WOOD DESIGN MERIT AWARD, 2005
INTERFAITH FORUM ON RELIGION, ART & ARCHITECTURE DESIGN
HONOR AWARD, 2007

CAPITOL HILL LIBRARY,
Seattle, Washington, 2003
(IN COLLABORATION WITH JOHNSTON ARCHITECTS)

Client: City of Seattle
Project Team: Jim Cutler, Ray Johnston of Johnston
Architects, Bruce Anderson, Marc Peveto,
Matthew Bissen
Structural Engineer: Swenson Say Faget
Civil Engineer: Rosewater Engineering
M/E/P Engineers: McGowan Broz Engineers
Landscape Architect: Nakano Architects
Interior Design: Nancy Burfiend, NB Design
Artist: Iole Allesandrini
Contractor: Summit Central Construction
Photographer: Art Grice

LONG RESIDENCE,
Orcas Island, Washington, 2003

Client: Dixon and Ruthanne Long
Project Team: Jim Cutler, Julie Cripe,
Chad Harding
Structural Engineer: DeAnn Arnholtz
at Coffman Engineers
Contractor: Alford Homes
Photographer: Art Grice
AIA/SUNSET/WESTERN HOME MERIT AWARD, 2005–06
WOOD DESIGN HONOR AWARD, 2004
AIA SEATTLE MERIT AWARD, 2004

A NEW JOINT PORT OF ENTRY,
Oroville, Washington, and
Osoyoos, British Columbia, Canada, 2004

Client: U.S. General Services Administration, Region 10,
Auburn, Washington, and Canada Customs and Revenue
Agency, Ottawa, Canada
Project Team: Jim Cutler, Pat Munter; from Bassetti
Architects: Rick Huxley, Michael Thorpe, John Jeffcott
Associated Architects: Bassetti Architects, Meiklejohn
Architects
Landscape Architect: Verdigris Landscape Architects
Civil Engineer: White Shield
Structural Engineer: KPFF Consulting Engineers
Mechanical Engineer: The Greenbusch Group
Electrical Engineer: Interface Engineering
Contractors: United States side: Intermountain Construction, Derek Wright, Project Manager, and Eric Reese,
Superintendent; Canadian side: Greyback Construction,
Larry Kenyon, Project Manager, and Gilber Thore,
Superintendent
Photographer: Art Grice

FLINT BEACH RESIDENCE,
Lopez Island, Washington, 2004

Client: Tom and Sally Reeve
Project Team: Jim Cutler, Janet Longenecker
Contractor: Russet Construction, Brett Ackerman,
Head Framer
Photographer: Art Grice

MALLORCA RESIDENCE,
Puerto Andratx, Mallorca, Spain

Client: Private
Project Team: Jim Cutler, Debra Cedeno
Contractor: Gossica Construction, Pepe Padanes,
Partner in Charge
Photographer: Art Grice

STUDIO, GUESTHOUSE, AND MAIN RESIDENCE
AT METEOR VINEYARDS,
Napa, California, 2005

Client: Private
Project Team: Jim Cutler, Bruce Anderson, Janet Longe-
necker, Debra Cedeno, Hiroki Kurozumi, Webster Wilson,
Sam Hanna, David Wagner, Michael McAllister
Structural Engineer: Craig Lee, DeAnn Arnholtz at
Coffman Engineers
Vineyard Specialist: Mike Wolf at Vineyard Services
Contractors: Cello & Maudru Construction (studio and
guesthouse), Tanglefoot Master Builders (main residence
and guesthouse)
Photographer: Art Grice

ORLEAN GILLESPIE RESIDENCE,
Gallatin, New York, 2005

Client: Susan Orlean and John Gillespie
Project Team: Jim Cutler, Janet Longenecker
Contractor: Prutting and Company Custom Builders
Photographer: Art Grice

OHANA HOUSE AT NIULII,
North Kohala, Island of Hawaii, Hawaii, 2005

Client: Private
Project Team: Jim Cutler, Janet Longenecker, Hiroki
Kurozumi
Contractor: Clayton Turnbull
Photographer: Art Grice
    AIA SEATTLE MERIT AWARD, 2006
    WOOD DESIGN CITATION AWARD, 2006

SPRING CREEK RANCH GOLF HOUSE,
Collierville, Tennessee, 2007

Client: The Meyer and Stanford Families
Project Team: Jim Cutler, Pat Munter
Consultants: KPFF Consulting Engineers, MacDonald-
Miller Facility Solutions, Travis Fitzmaurice & Associates
Contractor: Linkous Construction Company, W. A.Soefker
Mechanical Engineer: Gusmus Electric
Photographer: Art Grice

PURCHASE, NEW YORK, RESIDENCE,
Purchase, New York, 2007

Client: Private
Project Team: Jim Cutler, Bruce Anderson, Debra
Cedeno
Contractor: Prutting and Company Custom Builders
Photographer: Art Grice

FURNITURE AND HARDWARE

With the exception of the Orlean Gillespie fireplace tools,
Cutler Anderson's furniture and hardware is available
through Reveal Designs, White Plains, New York.
www.reveal-designs.com

Photographer: Art Grice

ABOUT THE ARCHITECTS

James L. Cutler, FAIA, was born in 1949 in Wilkes-Barre, Pennsylvania. He earned a bachelor of arts (1971) and a master's in architecture (1973) at the University of Pennsylvania and earned a second master's in architecture from the Louis I. Kahn Studio Program (1974). He received a Dale Fellowship (a traveling fellowship for design excellence), the James Smythe Turner Prize, and the Edward Spayed Brooke Medal.

Since 1977, he has been principal of his own design firm, Cutler Anderson Architects (formerly James Cutler Architects), on Bainbridge Island, Washington. He has served as a critic and design instructor at the Universities of Washington, Pennsylvania, and California at Berkeley (Friedman Professorship, 1999) and at Harvard University's Graduate School of Design, and was the Pietro Belluschi Distinguished Visiting Professor at the University of Oregon (1999).

Cutler was "Artist in Residence" at Dartmouth College, Hanover, New Hampshire, in the spring of 2004. In August of 2005, he served as chair of and hosted the AIA Central States Region Design Awards jury. In the spring of 2006, he returned to Dartmouth to teach studio art.

Bruce E. Anderson, AIA, was born in 1959 in Seattle, Washington. He earned a bachelor of arts (1981) and a master's in architecture (1988) from the University of Washington, where he also received the Architecture Faculty Design Medal and was elected to Tau Sigma Delta Architecture Honor Society. He began working with James Cutler in 1982 and became a partner in 2001. He has served as a critic and instructor at the University of Washington, as chair of the City of Bainbridge Island Planning Commission, and as president of the Bainbridge Island Land Trust, a nonprofit corporation that has protected more than a thousand acres of wildlife habitat.

He was also a guest critic at the 2004 Bowman Design Forum in Manhattan, Kansas, and at Jim Cutler's 2006 studio art class at Dartmouth College in Hanover, New Hampshire. He recently participated in a panel discussion on the future of architecture at the International Architectural Roundtable in Vancouver, British Columbia, Canada.

Photograph by Marc Anderson

From the front: Dunja Pelto, Susan Valentine, Keegan Furfaro, Vikki Anderson, Pat Munter, Zack Gillum, Janet Longenecker, Amy Koenig, Rebecca Dixon, Bruce Anderson, David Curtin, Brian Hegstad, Sean Haste, Jim Cutler, Kyle DeHaven

ABOUT THE AUTHORS

Sheri Olson, FAIA, is an architect and architecture critic. She was a contributing editor to *Architectural Record* and a columnist for the *Seattle Post-Intelligencer*. She is the author of *Miller/Hull Architects of the Pacific Northwest* and *Cutler Anderson Architects* (Rockport, 2004).

Alicia Kennedy is a writer and design editor. She was a founding editor of the architecture journal *Assemblage*. She is currently working on a book about prefabricated environments for *Contemporary Design in Detail* (Rockport, 2007–09), of which she is series editor.

Theresa Morrow is a Seattle-based journalist. She has written for publications nationally and internationally and was a contributor to *James Cutler* (Rockport, 1997).